CLAIMING THEOLOGY IN THE PULPIT

CLAIMING THEOLOGY IN THE PULPIT

BURTON Z COOPER

AND

JOHN S. MCCLURE

Westminster John Knox Press
LOUISVILLE • LONDON

Book design by Sharon Adams
Cover design by Eric Walljasper, Minneapolis, MN

First edition
Published by Westminster John Knox Press
Louisville, Kentucky

This book is printed on acid-free paper that meets the American National Standards Institute Z39.48 standard. ∞

PRINTED IN THE UNITED STATES OF AMERICA

03 04 05 06 07 08 09 10 11 12 — 10 9 8 7 6 5 4 3 2 1

Library of Congress Cataloging-in-Publication Data is on file at the Library of Congress, Washington, D.C.

ISBN 0-664-22702-3

To Blanche and Annie,
our companions in life and faith

I turned to speak to God
About the world's despair
But to make bad matters worse
I found God wasn't there.

God turned to speak to me
(Don't anybody laugh)
God found I wasn't there—
At least not over half.

Robert Frost

Contents

Preface

*T*his book had its beginnings in a lunchroom discussion between a theologian and a homiletician. The theologian was complaining about the seeming irrelevance of his discipline to church preaching. "I have a hard time recognizing my own students when I hear them preach," he said, "and the only theology I hear on Sunday mornings comes from biblical commentaries." The homiletician replied, "Let's teach a course that does something about that."

That course was designed and taught for several years at Louisville Presbyterian Theological Seminary. Our goal was to bring a preacher's theological knowledge and perspective—whether it be Barthian, Tillichian, Moltmannian, Rahnerian; liberationist, feminist; Catholic, Protestant, or Orthodox; conservative or liberal; pluralist or exclusivist—to bear upon biblical texts, and questions or issues arising from the world. Our means was a theological typology, from which preachers could extract their particular theological profiles, and through which a class of preachers could engage in sermon preparation and analysis sessions. The original ten-page theological typology has now been greatly revised and extended. It constitutes part 1 of this book and was written by Burton Cooper. Extracts from a transcript of class sessions, with extended commentary on the use of the typology for homiletical purposes, constitute part 2 of the book, which was written by John McClure. In addition, there is a chapter containing two sermons, in which Cooper and McClure typologically analyze each other's sermon. Finally, the book contains both a short form and a chart of the theological typology.

We owe thanks to many people. First, to all the students and ministers in our "Theology and Preaching" classes, especially to the seven who came to our one-week seminar in a renovated Vermont barn and graciously gave us permission to publish and comment upon their discussions. Those seven are: The Reverends Leslie Belden, Elizabeth Hinson-Hasty, Lee Hinson-Hasty, Dwight McCormick, Mitch Trigger, Sue Trigger, and Steve Van Kuiken.

Thanks to Gunnar Urang, retired priest and former college professor, who read each typological category as it came off the computer and engaged its author in critical discussions over fish sandwiches and reubens at the Fairlee Diner in the Vermont hills. Thanks also to Stephen Cooper, Associate Professor of Religious Studies at Franklin and Marshall College, who saved the manuscript from many an embarrassing phrase, editing the whole of part 1 with a scrupulousness that only a son could bring to a father's work. We also appreciate the wisdom and insight of Amy Pauw and Earl Koopercamp, who reviewed several portions of the manuscript. Finally, thanks to our wives, Annie McClure and Blanche Cogswell Cooper, to whom we have dedicated this book.

Corinth, Vermont
Louisville, Kentucky

PART 1   # The Theological Profile

Preliminary Remarks

*O*ur reason for writing this book is to improve preaching. To accomplish this goal, we focus upon a factor in the sermon that is at once central to preaching and yet, for reasons peculiar to our fractured and pluralistic times, has become increasingly difficult to achieve: a clear and consistent theological perspective in the content of the sermon. This book proposes to do something about that. It provides a method that clarifies a preacher's operative theological perspective and the differing perspectives of others, especially, though not only, those in the preacher's own congregation. Such clarification can enrich the interpretation of biblical texts and promote theological connectedness across the range of a preacher's sermons.

Theological knowledge in itself does not make a good preacher. Plenty of theologians are mediocre preachers. We are not talking simply about academic knowledge of theology, but about the kind of theological knowing that lies implicit in the worldviews, commitments, and actions of the preacher, and in the beliefs and life practices of members of the congregation. When preachers gain awareness of this kind of knowledge, their theological consciousness is intensified, and this, we have discovered, leads to more effective preaching. This, then, is precisely what we propose to do: intensify the preacher's theological consciousness.

Congregations respond appreciatively, even enthusiastically, to good preaching. Mainline denominational churches have a history of expecting preaching that combines conviction with critical theological reflection. The failure of preaching to meet this (historical) expectation contributes to the current malaise of these churches. We are not unaware of the sociological data suggesting the relative unimportance of preaching in today's church. But that data may reflect nothing more than the laity's realistic response to the current state of preaching. We contend that theologically improved preaching will contribute to the revitalization of the church for this reason. The sermon, in principle, is central to the life and thought of a worshipping community. It brings together the fundamental working powers and authorities of a living faith. In the context of a worship service, the sermon is the meeting place of God, Scripture, and the present; it provides a home for faith, theology, and culture; it is where a biblical understanding of reality is confessed, interpreted, and related to our experience of reality; it is where we hear whispered to us an inner word of God addressing the particularities of our lives and times; and, finally, it is where gospel and judgment encounter us.

Preaching presupposes faith, both the faith of the preacher and the faith, or at least the openness to faith, of the hearer. The importance of a sermon conveying the preacher's faith conviction, without calling attention to it, cannot be overestimated. The reason lies in the nature of religious faith. Our faith in God and Christ lies at a deeper, more personal level than our explicit beliefs and ideas can express. Our love of God, our trust in God, our felt need of God, our loyalty to God, in other words, our emotional relatedness to God, lie at a more fundamental level than our ideas about God. The language of preaching, then, must meet our faith on both the conceptual and emotional levels. It must have in view not simply the instructing of our understanding but the stimulating and even directing of our religious feelings. Of course there are abuses of emotion in the religious life, but we do not solve such problems by making religion more rational than it is. The sermon needs to express the felt depth of faith in order to engage the religious passions of the congregation. It cannot do this apart from conveying the preacher's deeply felt faith. The religious passions are the springs of a living faith; and a sermon lives in touching our passions.

Having said that, we must not forget that theology, too, is presupposed in preaching. A sermon is not simply a witness to the passions of one's faith; it also involves rational and critical reflection upon that faith. This brings us to the difficulty of distinguishing between theology and faith. These two are so intertwined that it sometimes seems as if the contents of my theology, my religious ideas, constitute my faith and my passion. This is because the simplest statement of faith can imply a vast theology and, at a minimum, invites a theological discussion. When we confess God as our creator or Christ as our redeemer we are confessing our faith, that is, our trust in God as the loving source of our being, but we seem also to be confessing a theology of creation and redemption, implying an array of ideas about providence, sin, repentance, sacrifice, resurrection, eternal life, and so forth. Yet we know that although we remain people of faith, the particulars of our theological convictions can and do change, both in our own personal history and in the history of the church. We may think of our faith as ultimate, but surely not our theology. How then can we clarify the distinction?

Instead of approaching the problem conceptually, let us start with a story. Some years ago, I was walking in the Vermont woods, climbing a steep hill on an old logging road that I had not walked before. Near the top of the hill was a bend in the road and then a clearing, so that as I came to it a view of the entire river valley opened up below me. Vermont river valleys, at least in the eastern part of the state, are relatively narrow, but they can be breathtaking in their beauty. Perhaps because the opening on the road was unexpected and the change of view was so sudden, the beauty of the landscape overwhelmed me. I was stunned, flooded with feelings, dizzy from them, and I found myself reaching for words; but other than dumbly to repeat that it was beautiful, I could not say why this scene so exhilarated me, so filled me with pleasure. I had the passion but not the understanding—at least, not much understanding. I suppose that now, on reflection, I could say something about color and line and contrast, but even so, my feelings would be totally out of proportion to my words. Yet, though my understanding of beauty remains small, the beauty of Vermont's hills and valleys means much to me, so much so that I bought a home and land in Vermont in order to live in its midst.

The irony of my decision to live in Vermont, rooted as it is in felt passions, felt apprehensions, perceptions that are emotionally rich and not merely cognitive, does not escape me, for I have lived my adult life as a professional theologian devoted to concepts, to analysis, to explanation, to arguments. But this irony suggests a way of clarifying the distinction between faith and theology. For the truth is, I do not leave unexamined my felt apprehensions of Vermont's beauty. Of course I know that the fundamental thing is the experience of beauty, yet I regularly ask myself what is it that I see that gives me so much pleasure. As I get answers to that question, I learn to look for certain things as I walk along old roads and woodland trails, thereby intensifying my sense of the beauty of my surroundings. I am exemplifying Yogi Berra's oft-quoted comment that you can see a lot by looking. It is similar with faith. The fundamental thing is the felt apprehension of God's care for us, God's mercy toward us, God's spiritual empowering of us, and so forth. But I do not leave unexamined these felt apprehensions. I ask questions about them—for I participate in the fundamental human activity of asking questions about my experiences, even, perhaps especially, my religious experiences. The questions, and the lifelong struggle toward answers, help me to see better into the ways of God's presence in the world, thereby deepening my apprehension of God. Of course, the lure of the analysis, carried too far, can tempt us to lose sight of the underlying experience—and that, too, from time to time, has happened to me. Still, we do not solve the problem of the reflective and analytical aspect of religion by making it less rational than it is. Faith, and the life of faith, is fundamental, and theology only matters in so far as it enhances and deepens our faith and our lives. Even so, we do not have our faith apart from theological reflection.

Theology, then, is essential but not prior; it presupposes the faith of the individual and the confessing community. In Paul Tillich's happy image, we already stand in the circle of faith when we find ourselves thinking theologically. Theology is faith articulating itself, faith coming to consciousness of itself. It is the work of a faith community, the church, seeking to understand itself, its convictions, and the relation of those convictions to important social and political issues in its life. Theology is also critical of itself; that is, critical of its previous articulations. This is because theological thinking occurs in history and, therefore, has a history. The theological expression of any given faith community reflects the universal ground of faith and the general limits of human understanding. But it also reflects the relativities and limits of the particular historical perspective and culture of that community's time and place. God is universal; so in faith we stand assured that we experience, participate in, and witness to the universal. But we are finite, historical beings, time bound and culture bound; we can only experience and express the universal through the lens of our history-culture-formed being. As H. Richard Niebuhr reminds us in *The Meaning of Revelation*, "It is one thing to have a view of the universal; it is another to claim universal views." To recognize this difference is to understand the distinction between faith and theology— an understanding that is especially important for the church today as it seeks to deal with the diversity and change in its history, with current denominational differences, and with the relation of Christianity to other world religions. But it is also important for the preacher, who every week faces a theologically diverse congregation in an ideologically and religiously diverse world.

Much has been written, these past fifty years, on the increasing biblical illiteracy of the mainline denominational churches, and its detrimental effects on the life of the church. There is widespread agreement that the church needs to educate itself biblically. But it is equally important for the church to address the increasing theological diversity within its congregations. We are referring to the diversity of ideas that arise when church members are encouraged to express their views on theological doctrines such as God's power, Christ's nature, the problem of evil, the afterlife, the authority of the Bible, the meaning of salvation, and so on; also, to the variety of implicit theologies signified in believers' different life styles, ethical decisions, and social commitments. In socially quiet times, perhaps, a church will pay no great price for ignoring the diversity of beliefs present in her congregations. But when the church is troubled by difficult social issues—such as abortion; racism; war; capital punishment; the ordination of women, gays, and lesbians; the use of inclusive language in worship; the relation of Christianity to other religions (Judaism, Islam, etc.); the place of prayer in our public schools; the teaching of creationism in the classroom—then moral and theological diversity can lead to bitter conflict and church division.

The solution to the problems inherent in diversity is not simply a matter of education. Theology today is highly pluralistic—for a score of reasons, many of them justifiable and unavoidable—so that theological education would only make explicit, and perhaps further, the theological diversity present, though largely hidden, in today's congregations. Also, the preacher in a mainline denominational church is not the exception to that diversity but its exemplar. Preachers have not only come out of the churches whose diversity they reflect, but they are also exposed in seminary to the theological pluralism that marks the current state of theology. Seminaries are not likely to lose their pluralistic character. Even if that could be accomplished politically, the price would be too high: church division and the loss of scholarly integrity.

The beginning of an answer, at least on the level of homiletics, lies in preachers identifying—that is, becoming conscious of—their particular theological perspective in contrast to other perspectives, and also becoming aware of the range of theological perspectives that are present, implicitly and explicitly, in their congregations. Different theological perspectives lead to different interpretations of biblical texts, different ways of responding to social issues, and consequently different ways in which individual members of a congregation interpret and assess a sermon. The preacher's awareness of these differences and their consequences can help to mitigate misunderstandings of the sermon, provide the basis for an attitude of respectful engagement with divergent positions on theological and social issues, and widen the reach and positive power of the sermon.

Of course, not all theological perspectives are equally adequate to particular church communities with their criteria of scriptural grounding, continuity with tradition, internal coherence, communal and individual experience, and so on. And some theological perspectives can be inappropriate to any Christian community. We are talking about theological pluralism, not theological relativism, about a plurality of valid theological interpretations and perspectives, not a toleration of all interpretations on the ground that there is no valid basis whatsoever to evaluate conflicting claims. It is one thing to say that there is more than one valid interpretation of a parable of Jesus or of the character of resurrected life; it is another thing to say that all interpretations have equal claim to validity. Similarly, in talking about the Roman Catholic or Lutheran or Reformed community, it is one thing to say that there is more than one form of theology that is a valid expression of the Roman Catholic or Lutheran or Reformed tradition, and quite another to say that all interpretations have a claim to validity.

Within the history of the church, we can locate a range of theological perspectives and interpretations of doctrines that, though differing from each other, and even in severe tension with each other, can make a claim for validity based on criteria recognized by the church as a whole. This range of theological positions provides the basis for the typology we have drawn up. The virtue of such a typology lies in providing a quick education into the church's theological diversity. It can make us more aware of our own doctrinal positions and particular theological perspective, and thus open our understanding to beliefs and attitudes alien to our own. It also can challenge and deepen our own thought. Of course, typologies suffer from the danger of insufficient depth, of oversimplification, and they can become destructive of their own ends when used to pigeonhole people. Even more, typologies can become too narrow in focus, refusing to recognize historically significant positions.[1] Worse still, they can be used to invoke invidious comparisons.[2] Our intent is to avoid these dangers; we have striven to be inclusive and evenhanded. Still, we know all too well that there is always a gap between intent and accomplishment—and that the reader can perceive this gap more readily than the writer.

The theological typology we propose offers eight categories in all. Three categories deal with our theological presuppositions, what we call "hidden determinants." They are: method, authority, and theistic worldview. The remaining five categories deal with consciously held doctrinal ideas. They are: theodicy, atonement, ethics and ecclesiology, the relation of Christianity to other religions, and eternal life/eschatology. Each category breaks down into three to five types. By locating one's theological type within each of the eight categories, a theological profile emerges—and one's theological awareness of self and others is intensified.

When a preacher's theological consciousness is heightened, theology takes on a more significant role in the interpretation of biblical texts and the analysis of the events, situations, and issues in one's time. Also, it encourages the preacher to deal sensitively and fruitfully with the range of theological alternatives that may be present in the congregation. Beyond its homiletic function, the typology can become the occasion for theological conversation between pastors and members of the congregation. In short, the typology is an interpretive and relationship-building instrument for a theologically diverse yet biblically grounded church.

As you read through the typology, make a note of the type (or types) in each of the eight categories to which you feel a theological kinship. Record your affinities on the Theological Profile Chart in appendix B. This is your initial theological profile ("initial" in that a theological consciousness is not set in concrete). Examine it for relative consistency of method and thought. Then proceed to part 2 where further instructions await you.

Chapter 1

The Hidden Determinants:
Method, Authority, and Worldview

*T*he word *theology* appears today in a variety of contexts, including secular ones, and its meaning varies from context to context. So, we need to clarify the meaning of theology in its Christian context. On one level, it is the articulation and interpretation of the beliefs that Christians affirm. These include but are not limited to: God the creator is a trinity of persons yet one reality; Christ is the Word made flesh, fully human and fully divine, the means of our redemption; human beings are created in God's image, free and finite, but have also come to be sinful; salvation is God's forgiveness and eternal life, and involves human repentance and faith in Christ's resurrection; the church is the body of Christ, the community of believers; the sacramental bread and wine are a means of grace and signify the body and blood of Christ; the Holy Spirit blows where it will. If a group of us listed our beliefs and then compared the lists, we would find much agreement; but as we talked about the meaning of these beliefs, differences in interpretation and emphasis also would appear.

In the next chapter, we will look at a range of doctrinal differences that lie in the history of the church's thought and, of course, in our own minds as well. But, first, we need to disclose another, hidden, level of our theology: the almost unquestioned assumptions we make that direct our thought one way or another. These are our presuppositions—sometimes conscious, sometimes unconscious—that account in part for the differences of interpretation that appear among us. We can get to this level of our theology by asking ourselves certain kinds of questions. Why do we give more weight to some biblical texts than to others? What counts, and what does not count, as an authority for our theological thinking? How do we conceive God's relation to the world? (Is the world essential to God? Do the world's actions change God in any way?) How do we account for theological perspectives different from our own? As we answer these questions and others like them, we are uncovering our theological method (including principles of interpretation), our epistemological authority, and our theistic worldview. These are the largely hidden determinants in our theological thinking. We all have them, though we do not necessarily have the same ones. The question is: Which ones are ours? Which ones are in the congregations to whom we preach? Which ones are in our denominational traditions? The typological analysis that follows leads us toward answers and opens up some new questions that spur our thought—in the interest of preaching.

The Four Basic Theological Modes

Were we to write a book on our faith containing all our theological beliefs, we would have to decide on a beginning point. What would be the first doctrine or topic or theme we would discuss? Why would we choose one starting point rather than another? Why do others choose other starting points? In the history of the church's thinking, we can identify four major entry points. Let us call them *modes,* for they are contrasting ways of thinking theologically. They all start at a different point because they differ in certain of their assumptions about the meaning of faith. We can signify each mode's distinctiveness by its title: the existential, the transcendent, the ethical-political (which has taken two forms in our times), and the relational. When we sense an intellectual kinship toward a particular mode, we are discovering—becoming conscious of—our basic theological perspective.

The modes, as I describe them, are pure types. Most of us are not pure in our thinking. We draw our ideas from diverse sources, and we do not worry overmuch about their inner coherence. After all, we tell ourselves, and rightly so, there is more to life than lies in our logic. We may feel that we only more or less fit in a mode, or we may feel a kinship toward more than one mode. That can mean there are some tensions, even contradictions, in our thought that we need to take account of, resolving some and consciously living with others. In learning why we live with some theological tensions—but not others—we allow them to become a good thing: the occasion for our own critical and creative thinking.

1. The Existential Mode

Here, theology begins with the experience of the negative, specifically with negative states of consciousness such as anxiety, loneliness, meaninglessness, guilt, despair, lack of worth, emptiness, and so forth. Of course, a negative consciousness can be triggered by some terrible objective event, such as a murder, a massacre, a rape, a debilitating illness, or a devastating fire, flood, or earthquake. But from the existential perspective, it is not the terrible event itself but a certain kind of reflection upon it that constitutes the theological entry point. When I am ill or when a loved one dies or when I lose my job, then I may certainly suffer, but not necessarily in the existential mode. Everything depends on how I respond inwardly to the negative event. I may recover from my illness, considering it an unfortunate accident, a deviation from the norm of health. Or I may think of the accidental death of a young loved one as a terrible event but still an unlikely one, a fluke, and push thoughts of death to the back of my consciousness. Or I may get a new job, and bask in the security it promises me. On the other hand, my illness, or even the illness of another, may lead me to reflect on the tenuous state of good health and the absence of any guarantees against my being stricken tomorrow by some devastating disease. The death of a loved one may lead me to see that those I love can die at any moment or, almost as bad, can cease to love me for reasons beyond my control. The loss of my job can show me that though I need work, work is not guaranteed to me or to anyone. Existence now appears perilous. Simply to live opens me to a host of dangers from which my talents and my social status offer no sure protection. I am full of questions that need reassuring answers. But the more I reflect, the less reassuring are my answers. I have discovered life in the existential mode.

Two words describe the character of the existential perspective: anxiety and despair. Perhaps, following Paul Tillich, we define anxiety best as: "finitude aware of itself." All creatures are finite, limited in a thousand ways; humans are conscious of their limits and of the perils consequent to finite existence. The source of the anxiety is not simply the perils but the nothingness that underlies them. No matter what I achieve, I can lose it, including life itself. Nothingness is an ever-present possibility. Nothing has to be, including me. No matter what I think or do, my understanding is finite, limited, so that I can be wrong or mistaken about things that matter the most to me. Nothing is certain. I am anxious about "nothing."

When I look within myself, or within humanity as a whole, for the resources to counter this anxiety about nothing, I do not find them. For all human resources are limited; and it is precisely these limits, and the consciousness of them, that are the source of anxiety. But with this discovery, my anxiety turns to despair. I am snared by the "Catch 22" of existence. My very love of existence intensifies my consciousness of life. The more consciousness, the more awareness of the underlying nothingness, and my ultimate powerlessness in relation to it, so that the human enterprise appears hopeless to me. I lose my love of existence, my desire to be, and, in that sense, I lose my self and fall into despair of ever being able to recover it. For this reason, Soren Kierkegaard calls despair the sickness unto death.

Kierkegaard also calls despair the entry hall to faith. He means that the first step toward faith in the redemptive power of God presupposes the self's loss of faith in its own resources to affirm and sustain itself in the face of death, suffering, the unknown, guilt, and sin. Those who have not personally experienced the depths of despair know neither the full meaning of human existence nor the full meaning of faith in God's power, especially God's redemptive power in Christ. God alone has the power to overcome the nothingness that underlies our despair, so that only a life characterized by faith in God is truly a life without despair.

William James provides the term *twice born* for those who move from despair to faith. He means that those who come to faith as the answer to despair have experienced both the death and the rebirth of the spirit. Shades of Nicodemus. There are some classic examples. The young Augustine, despite his considerable intellectual and spiritual gifts and a successful public career, increasingly found life futile and empty of meaning. The young Luther, despite his earnest efforts toward living an exemplary monastic life, and despite the assurances and encouragement of his superiors, increasingly lost hope of being worthy of God's salvation. Only when they reached bottom in their efforts to find a way to salvation did the occasion for genuine faith open to them.

In the existential mode, then, the creation is something that needs to be redeemed. Negativity, especially in the form of sin and death, shapes the underlying dynamics of human nature. There is, therefore, a universal human predicament: sin and death; and a corresponding universal human need: redemption and eternal life. We need to be redeemed and sustained, and we lack the resources to do so. We cry out to the universe for a power that has these resources. God is the infinite, spiritual power that can sustain the finite, sinful self in a broken and morally ambiguous world of suffering and death. Faith is the transition point. By virtue of faith, we find ultimate meaning so that our despair does not destroy us. Equally important, it is by faith that we find ourselves open to the Christian life of hope, forgiveness, repentance, humility, love of others, and gratitude to God—though brokenness and ambiguity remain even in the life of faith.

2. The Transcendent Mode

In this mode, theology begins with an absolute affirmation—namely, with God's saving action in Jesus Christ. So theology takes its starting point neither in human need nor in any inherent human sense of the divine, but in God's freely given, redemptive act in Christ. Scripture witnesses to the revelation of this act, thereby becoming the vehicle of God's saving word, Jesus Christ, to us today. Any other starting point than this revelation is considered illusory or futile, for the following reasons. On the one hand, God is sheer transcendence, meaning not only that God's being and acts are not conditioned by the creation but that God is free in relation to the divine nature. There is nothing necessary in God's being, so there is no way our reason can lead us to an understanding of God. God freely decides from eternity to love us, to act graciously toward us, to save us in Christ. We know this through the life, death, and resurrection of Christ—that is, through a particular divine-disclosing act in our history. On the other hand, we are finite creatures, limited in our powers and in our knowledge. Worse, we are sinful, and that sinfulness reaches so deep that we deceive ourselves into imaging God according to our needs and our ways of thinking. Our ideas and imaginations are distorted by our sinfulness—so nothing in our inner or outer experience would lead anywhere but to false belief or to unbelief. When we find ourselves thinking this way, we are thinking in the transcendent mode; we see it as a mistake, not an accidental mistake but a sinful, prideful mistake, to suppose a universal consciousness of God or even an awareness of a natural or given need for God. All talk of a "point of contact" between humanity and God is nothing more than the pretentious puffery of sin trying to make more of ourselves and our misdirected lives than is actually the case. Therefore, true knowledge of who God is and what God has done for us is possible only through particular, revelatory acts of God in our history.

In this way, the transcendent mode moves from an uncompromising negation of the human reach for God to an absolute affirmation of God's reach for humanity. For it is not simply that God has redeemed us in Christ, great as that news is, but that this is a gratuitous act, an act of sheer freedom, sheer love, on God's part. Nothing in the divine nature or in the creation necessitates God's decision to save us and to reveal that salvation to us. There is nothing even in us that looks or asks for it; we not only lack knowledge of our destiny, we lack awareness of the full depth of our sinful state. The knowledge of our sinfulness comes with the knowledge of our redemption, not before it. In the strongest sense possible, all the glory for our redemption belongs to God. God decrees from eternity the conquest of sin and death so that our destiny might be eternal life. Our part in the redemptive process is to respond with gratitude in our life and worship, including, especially, the proclamation of the good news to others.

Three traditional theological terms characterize the transcendent mode: *sola fides, solo Christo,* and *sola scriptura.*

Sola fides ("by faith alone") has a pastoral and theological meaning. Pastorally, it reassures us of God's love if only we have the faith to believe it. Such faith frees us from the anxiety of having to deserve salvation. There are no conditions we have to meet. God loves us out of divine grace, not out of some merit on our part. This is the deep theological meaning underlying Luther's famous essay on the freedom of the Christian. The Christian is free from having to earn God's love. Luther hastened to add that the Christian is also servant to all. But our servanthood, our willingness to meet the needs of others, is our grateful response to God's love, not a condition for it. In the life of faith, we may well remain a sinner. Even so, we know in faith that ultimately our sins are not held against us. We are saved by our faith.

Solo Christo ("by Christ alone") means it is in a particular act, in Christ, that God saves us, and it is through Christ's life that our salvation is revealed to us. God provides humanity with the bridge of Christ, over which all may come. Karl Barth's transcendentalism takes this almost to universalism: God, from eternity, elects all humanity in Christ; this is the good news revealed to us in Christ and which we are to preach through Christ.

Sola scriptura ("by Scripture alone") suggests that it is through Scripture, its reading and proclamation, that Christ is revealed to us and our faith engendered. It is the way God speaks to us. To say *sola scriptura* is to establish the authority of Scripture above other authorities such as reason, experience, and tradition. Pushed to its furthermost point, it may even exclude other authorities.

In the transcendent mode, then, the sovereignty of God dominates. God destines us from eternity, through God's action in Christ, to be conquerors of the negativities of the creation; sin and death will be no more. That is our inheritance. It is God's free gift to us. Therefore, the Christian life is one of joy, certainty, gratitude, proclamation, mission.

3. The Ethical-Political Mode

In this mode, faith and social commitment are interfused. Faith does not know itself apart from a commitment to social justice. Faith takes its self-understanding from the biblical witness to God's merciful love and justice, God's concern for and involvement in history, and God's purpose to bring human life into a just social order. The life of faith is polar, double ended, with inner convictions and social actions playing upon each other. The truth or depth of faith lies in its consequences for action, and the truth or depth of action lies in the inwardness of faith's convictions. If we do not love our brothers and sisters enough to work for a just social order for all, then we neither love our brothers and sisters nor do we have faith in God's promise of a coming kingdom. Similarly, doctrinal formulations are guided by concern for their relevancy to the practice and structures of social justice. The converse also is true: There is concern for the way certain traditional doctrines can perpetuate injustice.

In the twentieth century, two distinct forms of the ethical-political mode appeared: the social gospel and the liberationist.

The Social Gospel Form. Here, theology begins with the kingdom of God as the realizable and ultimate goal of history. History finds meaning in its movement to the kingdom—that is, to a just social order of brothers and sisters under God. We find meaning in our lives by participating in those causes that work to bring about God's kingdom. God's will works through the spirit and practice of our lives. Moral effort and the reform of social structures are jointly called for, and moral renewal is an ever-present possibility for each individual and for every society.

The origin of sin is social, lying in the social conditions and social systems in which people find and pursue their lives. For example, the root of even the personal vices—alcoholism, drug abuse, marital infidelity, lying, stealing—would be traced to an overly competitive, unstable economic system; a glaringly inegalitarian class system; an unjust legal system; or an inept, discriminatory educational system. Similarly, the supra-personal forces of evil—such as racial, ethnic, and religious hatred; the degradation of grinding poverty and ignorance; and the murderous fever that grasps warring nations—are embedded in the destructive dynamics of the social structures themselves. In this view, the church must critically examine society's political, economic, legal, educational, and military systems, uncovering their negative powers and calling for their reform so they work for justice and the common good.

Christ is the great teacher, the great exemplar, above all, the great inspirer, the one who calls us to tranform our lives both personally and socially. His moral teachings signify the ethic of the kingdom of God toward which we are called. His forgiveness of our sins removes the guilt and paralysis of our past so that we are free to turn our energies to God's mission now. That mission, God's kingdom, advances wherever Christ's spirit of love supersedes the use of force and legal coercion and wherever the principle of justice works to reform our social structures. The church is the corporate incarnation of the spirit of Christ and as such must take the lead in society in condemning all wrongs and in rallying social and political forces toward appropriate reforms. Both church and individual find their faith tested by its effectiveness in leading to the kingdom of God. The Christian life is one of steady and hopeful involvement in the reforming of social and political structures.

The Liberationist Form. In this form, theology begins with a commitment to stand with an oppressed people in their struggle against injustice—with African Americans as they fight racism and poverty, with women as they fight sexism and secondary status, with gays as they fight job discrimination and homophobia, with Hispanics as they fight poverty and ethnic discrimination, and so on. This commitment is grounded both in a personal revulsion against the suffering inflicted upon a people and in the faith that God works through us to end this suffering. It is the commitment that drives a person toward a liberation theology perspective, not the other way around. The commitment is always specific: it is to take one's stand with a particular community. A liberation theology takes its cue from that specificity: to analyze and criticize the particular forms of injustice oppressing that community, to give public and published voice to the way the oppressed group experiences its social reality, to work to recover the history of the community. This specificity of commitment and content accounts for the multiple forms of liberation theology: black theology, feminist theology, (Latin American) liberation theology, womanist theology (African American women), minjung theology (the Korean poor). Every oppressed community has a different history, lives under different conditions, and requires different strategies to overcome oppression and different means to energize and renew the spirit of the people.

There are, of course, common themes that inform all the liberation theologies. God is just and therefore sides with the poor against the oppressor; the unjust structures in the world defy God's intention; God's will and power are identified not with what is but with what will be; hope is a major category of faith, hope for change, hope as the source of joy, hope as the impetus for prayer and thanksgiving; growth in faith involves "conscientization," the valuing of self according to God's valuation rather than society's; social oppression is the major expression of sin, so that the dominant human predicament is the massive oppression by the powerful of the poor and the socially marginalized; the oppressor-oppressed structure of society, which forms the basis for social injustice, is to be replaced by non-hierarchical structures; the church is a community of faith and hope, a spiritual support for the poor and oppressed, and an agent of social change; Christ is the liberator who identifies with "the least," thereby including "the least" in God's kingdom; the kingdom, or the reign of God, is primarily conceived under the image of "a new heaven and a new earth," thereby undergirding our hopes and prompting us toward the transformation of our social structures as we know them. In sum, the Christian life of the liberationist is one of identification with an oppressed community and dedication to overcoming the structures that cause that oppression.

4. The Relational Mode

Here, theology begins with the experience of belonging. We sense our belonging to each other, to our community, to nature, and to God. We sense the connectedness of all things, the interwoven relationality of all aspects of the creation, the presence of the infinite in the finite, even a pre-reflective, felt presence of God in our innermost being. The religious life stems from God's communion or participation in all things—and our experience of that divine participation. It is not surprising, therefore, for those who think in the relational mode to find religion wherever we find human life: a religious consciousness comes with our humanity. Even so, a sinful consciousness comes, also. Sin is defined socially: the denial of our belongingness, a closing off from others, a rent in our relational being. Sin draws lines between those whom we care about and those whom we do not, between that part of existence which we are concerned to build up and that part to which we are indifferent or even hostile. We find ourselves born into a world of broken relations, living among a people whose history invariably includes hatred and violence, whether as victims or perpetrators or both. We inherit this history and the distrust of others that follows from it. In the course of our lives, some of us may work our way out of this distrust; others may simply reaffirm it. Still, even the best of us, in countless ways—whether out of selfishness, insecurity, false pride, or ignorance—commit acts that deny what is deepest in us: our essential belongingness to all that has being, including the ground of all being.

Two basic categories define this mode of thinking: *relationality* and *process*. To be is to be in relation. We are individuals in a social context. I owe my very beginnings, biological and psychological, to a network of social relations. My personal identity, which is mine alone, does not come to me apart from the particular world, the particular community, in which I find myself. The "I" that is "I" would be other if I were born in a different time, in a different place, in a different culture, or to different parents of a different class or of a different religion, race, or ethnic group. It matters how others respond to me and I to them because in a relational world, all actions have consequences for all, for better or worse—that is, for an increase or decrease in freedom, justice, harmony, creativity, and interest. The relational character of the world produces a multiple factor in the presence and power of sin. Sinful actions, actions that are heedless of their negative consequences on other individuals and groups, multiply not only through space but through time, as the history of the people who live in the Balkans, the Middle East, Northern Ireland, and the Indian subcontinent so amply and sadly demonstrates—let alone our own racial history in the United States.

The second basic category is process. Our mode of existence is dynamic. To be is to become; it is to be caught up in a process of creativity and change. The world is a place of becomings, of developing new forms and structures, where the self, as agent, participates in the dynamic, developmental character of being, not simply realizing innate potentials but creating new possibilities for itself. One's life is a history of responses to new situations and possibilities of being. It is a history of transformation amidst recurring characteristics. We are thinking in the relational mode when we root our identity not in some underlying, unchanging substance but in a developmental process that drives toward the new while allowing for and affirming continuity. I remember my past, but I do not know myself as the same person I was at two years of age, or at ten, or at twenty or thirty. Yet I recognize myself as myself no matter what my age, because I remember this past as my past and because there is continuity in it. The decisions I made were my decisions. Of course, the past sets limits to what I can do or become, but within those limits I can still experience significant freedom. And though my social inheritance—the character and history of the community into which I came to life—is a given, my response to it is not. Further, the past, both my own and my community's, can be such as to encourage my sense of responsibility, my openness to transformation, my search for wider harmonies, and my desire for justice for all peoples. A community does not simply set limits; it also sets possibilities, sometimes high ones. The communal home of the self can matter in the most positive of ways.

The relational mode affirms the church as "the mother of our faith." We become Christians in a community of Christians. The meaning and power of faith come to us through our participation in the life of a community seeking to be faithful to Christ's spirit. The sacraments signify this participatory-relational-experiential character of faith. Christ's body, broken for us, is received by us in the bread and wine, symbolizing our intent to open ourselves to Christ whose spirit is present in the worship of the church. The church is Christ's body; his spirit is one of loving concern for the other. When I go out in care to another, I say with Paul, "It is no longer I who live, but Christ who lives in me" (Gal. 2:20). That spirit defines the church and propels it ever outside itself, so that there are in principle no bounds to the relationality of the church. To all whom she encounters, the church says, sometimes aloud, sometimes to herself, "Christ died for you." This is the church in its essence. The actual life of the church is marked by ambiguity; it too is gripped by sin. Even so, the spirit of Christ can be discerned.

In a relational view, God is ever present, ever beckoning us to greater degrees of creativity and harmony. But much is also made of the ways that

God's relationality opens the door to divine suffering. God is the great participant, the loving companion to all life. God's suffering derives from God's love for us. Love suffers when the loved one suffers. We are approaching the central mystery of Christian faith: We do not have our redemption apart from divine suffering. The crucified and resurrected Christ is the great revelation of God's suffering, redemptive love for us. This revelation is like a forcefield, and from it God draws forth a new community, the church, whose power and essence is the spirit of Christ. Hence, the Christian life is heavily focused around both the worship and social outreach of the church.

Authority

We come now to another level of theological determinants: the authorities to which we turn, implicitly and explicitly, in formulating our beliefs. Historically, the church has recognized four types of authority: Scripture, tradition, experience, and reason. Of course, not all churches recognize all four authorities; even when they do, the authorities are not equally weighted—nor are there agreed-upon common definitions. We uncover our own authorities and their comparative weight in the ways we answer certain questions. Why do my beliefs strike me as true? What would convince me that a belief I hold is false? Why do some arguments seem persuasive, but not others? Why do some arguments convince others, but not me?

An illustration, taken from Dietrich Bonhoeffer's life and thought, clarifies how authorities shape and revise our beliefs. Bonhoeffer was a young but already influential German theologian when he published *The Cost of Discipleship* in 1937. Citing Matthew (5:38–42), Bonhoeffer argued that "According to Jesus . . . the right way to requite evil is not to resist it." This precept was for the church alone, for people of faith; it was not an ideal or general principle for the world as such. Bonhoeffer knew "that weakness and defencelessness invite aggression." He never tried to justify the precept by an appeal to experience or reason or tradition. Instead he appealed to the cross, and to the cross's power to "kindle a faith in the victory of suffering love over evil." On the strength of this faith, he argued, the follower of Christ practices nonviolence.[1]

This argument is straightforward Christian pacifism. There are no qualifiers, no conditions. It is based on particular New Testament texts: those commanding non-resistance to evil and those suggesting that we imitate Christ. Being a Christian means being transformed into the image of Christ.[2]

Bonhoeffer formulated those beliefs in the early years of the Nazi takeover of power in Germany. By 1939, however, he began to rethink his position. Hitler was implementing his anti-Jewish policies and plunging Europe into war. Bon-hoeffer was talking to leaders of the resistance movement. He now saw his paci-fism as an illegitimate escape from his Christian social and political responsibility. He formulated a crucial distinction between "arbitrary killing," which is taking the life of an innocent, and the wartime killing of an enemy engaged in attacking the lives of others.[3] Further, he practiced this change of belief—becoming active in the resistance movement, a movement whose prime goal was to assassinate Hitler. This activity cost him his life. He was imprisoned by the Nazi government and executed shortly before the end of the war.

Bonhoeffer's change of mind captures our imagination precisely because it cost him his life. We know he meant it. We know he could not have done it for light reasons. What were his reasons? What authority overruled his biblically based arguments for pacifism? Certainly, it was not that he accepted a higher authority than the Bible; it was more a matter of seeing aspects of Scripture not noted before, or at least not given much weight or value before. The "pacifist" texts were still there, as were Bonhoeffer's old pacifist arguments, but some-thing happened that gave more weight to other biblical texts and other argu-ments. That "happening" (or amalgam of happenings) was Hitler's policies and their destructive consequences. Scripture had not changed nor had it lost its authority, but Bonhoeffer now saw the texts of Scripture in the light cast by his experience of Nazi Germany. That experience became the occasion for a change in the way he interpreted biblical texts. Even so, nothing was neces-sary in his change of interpretation. Bonhoeffer's change of mind was more like coming to a new judgment than like drawing a logical conclusion, more like a member of a jury responding to a host of conflicting evidence and argu-ments than like a mathematician responding to the logic of numerical deduc-tions. There were, after all, Christian pacifists who, even in the face of Nazi horrors, did not revise their beliefs. The authorities that shape our beliefs do not operate coercively. There is an element of freedom in the ways we respond to them. This is true whether we are talking about the meaning of an experi-ence, the interpretation of a biblical text, or a pronouncement of the church on an article of faith. There is even an element of freedom in our choice of author-ities. But it is only an element. All of us have some authorities; we cannot do without them. We need them to find meaning and value in life, and we need to relate to them responsibly. We can do so by becoming aware of the complex-ity of ways authorities operate in our faith.

Those of us in the church confess the Bible as authoritative for our faith. But the Bible's authority is understood in a multiplicity of ways, allowing for a wide range of interpretations on almost any given issue—witness the dis-agreement in the church on such fundamental and varied areas as the theory of evolution, capital punishment, abortion, nonviolence, the role of women, the ordination of gays and lesbians, the doctrine of the Trinity, the resurrection, free will, the second coming of Christ, and a host of other issues and doctrines. There is no single reason for these disagreements. People belong to denominational churches, and the differing histories and theological traditions of denominations affect their thinking. Also, psychological, social, and cultural factors affect the interests, perspectives, and sympathies of the believer. Differences in experience, perspective, and tradition lead believers to assess differently the value and significance of particular biblical texts, so that there is disagreement on the weight to be given to one text in relation to another. For example, on the issue of women's roles, one person may find definitive the words on subordination found in the Epistles; others may take their clue from the suggestion in the Mary and Martha story that a range of roles is appropriate for women. Similarly, on the nature of Christ's resurrection, some may take their understanding from Paul's image of a "spiritual body" and his insistence that "flesh and blood" do not enter the kingdom; others may give more weight to the Emmaus story in Luke and the Thomas story in John, both of which suggest a more physical character to Christ's resurrected body.

Theological disagreement may also arise from contrasting ways of understanding the nature of a biblical text's truth. One believer might think of a text as literally true—for example, taking the Genesis accounts of the creation and fall as providing both scientific information about the order of creation and historical information about the first man and woman being expelled from the garden of Eden. Another believer might take those accounts symbolically, interpreting them as affirming the goodness of God's creation and the tendency of all of us to abuse our God-given powers, inevitably falling into sin. Of course, both believers would affirm the Bible as authoritative for their faith (especially when challenged, say, by a naturalist who finds no scientific grounds for divine purposes in the created order or by a post-modernist who "deconstructs" all arguments for objective meaning and value in the nature of things).

The following typology can help us become conscious of the particular way we understand the basis for the authority of Scripture and its relation to the other authorities: reason, tradition, and experience.

The Authority of the Bible: Four Types

There are four different ways the church conceives the Bible's authority. We can call them the way of verbal inspiration, the way of God's uniquely revealed word, the way of universal principles, and the way of God's fresh address.

1. The Way of Verbal Inspiration

Here, the Bible has authority because it is God-speech. The biblical writers are the inspired transcribers of that speech, the flute through which God plays the music. The Bible, then, is in principle inerrant, since God neither deceives nor errs. Still, there is the possibility of error in the process of transmission, so there are both "errantists" and "inerrantists" in this type. Scripture is typically interpreted literally: Eve was actually created from Adam's rib, Noah really lived to be hundreds of years old, Jonah lived three days inside the belly of a large fish, etc. On the other hand, not all words and stories need be taken literally—a biblical day of creation can be thought of as a thousand years. The Bible uses metaphor and Jesus talks in parables, which gives an opening for admitting figurative interpretations. Still, there is a plain meaning of the Bible. In matters of religious doctrines and morals, the words of Scripture, particularly those of the New Testament, are taken as absolutely true. Those words express God's transcendent perspective, not the relative perspective of the biblical transcriber, and therefore remain valid in all times and places.

2. The Way of God's Uniquely Revealed Word

Here, the Bible's authority rests on God choosing the culture, history, and language of ancient Israel and the early church to serve as a unique witness to divine revelation. Since revelation occurs in history and to a particular people, the words of Scripture reflect the particularism of their time and culture. In that sense, God's spiritual word is held in an earthen vessel. Even so, it is God's uniquely chosen vessel for revelation; it is the language used and given by God for God talk, and, therefore, is an irreplaceable expression of divine revelation. To change the language—other than through translation—alters the revelation so that it reflects our notions of God and gospel rather than God's self-revelation. Further, no metaphysic underlies the narratives and teachings of Scripture, such that the Bible could or should be translated into some particular philosophy of life or currently fashionable ideology. Rather, biblical language and narrative have inherent power to absorb and speak to any culture in any time and place. Human reason and experience, then, are strictly subordinate to the authority of Scripture. We are not to judge the truth of God's revelation by our past experience of reality, by the current assumptions and values of our culture, or by the rules and processes of rational thought.

3. The Way of Universal Principles

Here, the Bible's authority rests on the universal truths embedded in the texts of Scripture—to be uncovered via exegesis and interpretation. Scripture is understood as the originating documents of the Christian community. The documents, as a whole, witness to God's revelatory and redemptive presence in the history of an ancient people. Like all documents, they are historically conditioned; they reflect their time and place. For example, the Bible's picture of the cosmos reflects an ancient worldview, as does its patriarchal social system, its monarchial political system, and its agriculture-based economic system with its sanctioning of slavery. Therefore, it is necessary to distinguish the socio-cultural clothing of a text from its faith meaning. This can be done by rejecting beliefs that defy the bounds of reason and by identifying in any given text the universal in religious experience, moral value, and/or philosophic truth. The continuity of today's church with its biblical past is grounded, then, in common concepts generalized from biblical narratives and teachings, such as the oneness and mercy of God; God's care of the creation; God's concern for justice for all people, especially the weak and vulnerable; the command to love all our brothers and sisters; the church as a community for peace and reconciliation; and the belief in the resurrection of the body, or life after death.

4. The Way of God's Fresh Address

Here, the Bible's authority rests on a text's capacity to generate novel and multiple interpretations, thereby allowing Scripture to function as a vehicle for God's fresh and relevant address to the church. Scripture, then, is both God's past word and the means to hear God's present word. Though Scripture comes clothed in linguistic and conceptual expressions relative to other times and cultures, no text is to be dismissed or rejected outright on the grounds that it reflects merely the mores of an earlier culture, defies some general truth of reason, or seems to be unchristian. In principle, any text, via interpretation, can be a vehicle for a fresh word of God. Further, there is no such thing as a single correct meaning to each text. By bringing to old texts new questions from our own time; by interpreting each text in light of our current experience, understanding of nature, and worldviews; and by being conscious of the hermeneutic we bring to a text—whether it be liberationist, process, existentialist, or any other current and future interpretative schema—we allow the ancient texts to become vehicles of God's word to our world. The Christian truths that arise from interpretation are to be held firmly but provisionally. This is because Scripture is never through questioning our interpretations, is always opening itself to new interpretations, and stands in judgment over the new interpretations to which it opens itself. The church, then, is engaged in an ongoing critical dialogue between Scripture and interpretation. No text of Scripture is ever replaced by its interpretation. Even so, imperfect and provisional as the church's interpretations may be, that is the way the church hears God's current word.

The Authority of Tradition: Three Types

Tradition refers to that which has been handed down from the past to the present. In church usage, it can designate one or more of the following: historic creeds, confessions, doctrines, and declarations of church councils or assemblies; long-standing policies and practices, rites of worship, prayers, and symbols; and the classic or central theological heritage. A tradition's authority is the amount or kind of power that a past thought or action of the church has upon the church's present thought and action. That power can be deemed absolute—authorized for all times and places; or it can be deemed relative—authorized in the context or conditions of its origins. Absolutism pushed to an extreme would deny all power to new experience and new thought. Relativity pushed to an extreme would deny all power to tradition—because its relevancy is completely limited to its original time and place. There are three broad ways of understanding the authority of tradition. The tradition can be thought of as living, growing, developing, but without error (limited absoluteness); it can be thought of as seeking the relevant truth of faith in specific historical contexts (limited relativity); and it can be thought of as always relative to its social, psychological, and cultural context (absolute relativity). There is, at least in theory, a fourth possibility: sheer absoluteness. But this is only an abstract possibility; no thinker can completely prevent thoughts and experiences from their own time affecting their understanding of the tradition.

1. Limited Absoluteness

The church is guided into eternal truth by the Holy Spirit. This guidance can manifest itself in the church's official declarations, policies, and enduring practices. In principle, there can be traditions that are without error, and the church has the authority and obligation to declare them as absolute truths and practices. Even so, change is possible. No church ever grants absolute authority to all of its traditions; rather, it so authorizes only a limited number of traditions. Also, certain ways of understanding the development of ideas and practices allow for change by addition and qualification. Past teachings and practices could then be opened up, expanded upon, without denying their truth or relativizing them to some past era.

2. Limited Relativity

The Holy Spirit guides the church into truth, but that truth—whether it concerns doctrine, liturgical practice, or social justice issues—always emerges from and directs itself to a particular social and historical context. Changes in social conditions can make old truths irrelevant. For example, the church's past understanding of slavery, the place of women, the crusades to free the Holy Land, and the geocentric understanding of the universe can now be seen as grounded in social knowledge relative to its time. Other examples would be the medieval distinction of essence and property as a way to understand Christ's presence in the Eucharist; the church's resistance to evolutionary theory, expanding universe theory, theories of probability and randomness, etc.; and, most controversial of all, church traditions on abortion, euthanasia, suicide, and homosexuality. Those who hold this view do not deny that the tradition contains eternal truths. But they tend to uphold only the highly abstract truths: the church's concern for the poor, the understanding that God's grace extends to all people, the affirmation of the goodness of the creation, and so on. Equally significant, this view holds that changing social and political conditions can bring to light truths of the gospel that previously were in the shadows. Examples are strewn throughout the history of the church. Luther, confronted with the overbearing power of the traditions of medieval Christianity, emphasized the freedom granted by the gospel. Kierkegaard, facing impersonalized, Hegelian forms of theology, insisted on the subjective element in faith. The "social gospel" was the church's response to the economic devastation of the industrial revolution. Ecological theology's insistence on the relationality of all parts of God's creation is a response to the current dangerous exploitation of the resources of the earth. Liberation theology's emphasis on specific commitment to marginalized social groups and historically abused peoples arises out of a combination of modern social and political conditions that allowed a voice to those previously unvoiced.

3. Absolute Relativity

This view denies authority to the tradition. The denial has a classical and a (post)modern ground. The classical ground allows authority only to Scripture as a basis for religious truth. Here alone we find God's word to us. Any tradition of thought or practice, no matter how long established in the church, could be questioned on the basis of its adequacy to Scripture. Postmodernism sees all knowledge, including knowledge of God, as social knowledge; i.e., relative to time, place, culture, and even to class, race, gender, and ethnicity. Inadvertently, then, postmodernism's unqualified relativizing of all knowledge reinforces the argument of those who view Scripture as the only opening to eternal truths. If we are to be skeptical about all humanly achieved knowledge, then the only possibility for eternal truth lies in divinely revealed knowledge.

The Authority of Experience: Three Types

Experience is the medium by which we become aware of—take account of, gain knowledge of—realities outside and within ourselves. There is a tree in my backyard. How do I know that? Whenever I go out my back door, I see a tree: its green leaves, its branches, its trunk, its overall form. I can see it because my eyes pick up its image; that image, transmitted to the brain, I project upon a space in my backyard. In other words, I "know" there is a tree in my backyard because the tree in the form of its image enters into me through my eyes every time I exit my back door. That which is outside me has gotten inside me. I am experiencing it. On the authority of this experience—and, perhaps, the reinforcing experience of my sense of touch where I project the feeling of roughness and hardness on my fingertips onto the tree trunk to which my fingers are adjacent—I tell people that I have a tree in my backyard. If someone should say to me, "I never knew there was a tree in your backyard; I'm glad to hear that one is growing there," that person believes in the existence of my tree on the authority of my personal witness. Those who doubt my witness can come around to my backyard and see for themselves. Like Thomas in the gospel story, they come to belief only after they have seen or touched. They will then say that they believe on the authority of their own experience. Paul tells us that he persecuted the church until God "was pleased to reveal his Son to me" (Gal. 1:15–16; the Greek says, "in me"). Presumably, then, Paul would not believe in Christ's resurrection on the authority of the testimony of others, but only on the authority of his own experience of Christ. On the other hand, having accepted Christ's resurrection, he came to accept other teachings of the church on the authority of the tradition (1 Cor. 15:3–5).

I experience my tree; Paul experiences Christ. We use the same word, but the reference is to different modes of experiencing. The tree is a material reality; I experience it through sense perception. Anyone else standing where I stand would also perceive the tree. The tree is open to public perception. The risen Christ is a spiritual reality, open only to a private mode of experience. It has often been noted that Luke's two accounts of Paul's sensing of Christ's presence differ in their details of light and sound (Acts 9:7; 22:9). This does not mean Luke is confused about what happened. He is witnessing to Paul's spiritual experience of Christ—and is using the public language of sense perception to talk about Paul's private sensing of Christ confronting him. Analogously, experiences of the harmony of the universe, the connectedness of all things, the peace of God, the love of God, do not come to us via sense perceptions that would be experienced by another who happened to be standing where we are standing. They, too, are private and spiritual, not public and physical, experiences. When we hold that these spiritual experiences are feelings, intimations, of the way things are deep down, we are making two assumptions. The first is that physical reality—that which can be (publicly) perceived through the senses—does not exhaust reality, but that there is another level of reality, the spiritual level. The second assumption is that we have the (God-given) capacity to experience the spiritual level of reality.

Those who use experience as an authority for religious truth need to be wary of two problems. The first is our capacity for self-deception with regard to religious feelings. Some of our inner experiences, which have the feel of God to them, may have their source not in God's reality but in projected needs of our psyche. The second is our tendency to universalize our experience. If I experience God in such and such a way, then I assume all others can have the same experience and draw the same conclusion about God's nature as I do. Or, if my need for God is such and such, and God has answered that need, then I assume all others have a similar need, which God will answer. We do not always recognize that there is a multiplicity of human needs, that we differ among each other in terms of which needs dominate us, and that the way we experience God is shaped not only by who God is but by who we are. Universal statements may still be possible, but they need to take into cognizance the wide variety of human experiences of God.

Christians have three major options in regard to the authority of experience: the denial of all authority whatsoever (absolute denial), the denial of authority to experience prior to faith (relative denial), and the granting of some authority to human religious experience (relative affirmation).

1. Absolute Denial

Here, human experience lacks all authority in relation to religious knowledge. It is not a means to true and salvific knowledge of God, and provides only misleading or incomplete knowledge with regard to our nature and destiny. The reason is this: We have lost, never had, or have sinfully corrupted our capacity to experience the spiritual depth of reality. For such knowledge we are totally dependent upon God—that is, upon divine revelation. Revelation is found only in Scripture. Where it is asserted elsewhere (in the church, in a particular individual) it is by virtue of the power of the Holy Spirit speaking through our spirit, as a violin sounds its notes by virtue of the violinist.

2. Relative Denial

Here, experience has authority only within the context of faith. Apart from faith in Christ, sin corrupts our ability to experience God, leaving us unable to know God truly. We may have a sense of God, but it is a false or distorted sense because it is filtered to us through the sinful self. However, by God's grace, faith restores our capacity to know God rightly. In and through faith, we can experience God's forgiveness, God's love, God's judgment upon our lives, God's calling us to righteousness, and so on.

3. Relative Affirmation

Human life is created with the capacity to experience God. Sin clouds that capacity but does not destroy it. All of us are capable of a sense of God's presence, power, and love. In that sense, a general revelation of God is available through human experience. This general revelation is the basis for the existence of the world's religions. The differences among religions have to do with their origins, with the particulars of their historical and cultural foundations, with the course of their histories, and with the spiritual depth and dominant insights of their leaders.

The Authority of Reason: Five Types

The relation of faith to reason has been a contentious issue in the church from its beginning, and remains so today. Liberals, conservatives, moderates, and fundamentalists have different understandings of the role of reason in interpreting the faith of the church. *Reason* refers to rational modes of thinking as a way of gaining true knowledge about things. These modes are either deductive (reasoning abstractly from an unquestioned proposition to its logical conclusions) or inductive (reasoning from bits of data or evidence to a general or inclusive proposition). If I notice that my plants die when I do not water them, and if I conclude from this evidence that plants need water to live, I am reasoning inductively. If I begin with the proposition that heavy objects fall to the ground, and if I conclude from this abstract statement that my plants will fall downward if I push them off the shelf, then I am thinking deductively. In our deductive pursuit of truth, there are techniques of logical analysis that help us uncover contradictions in our thinking so that the truths we affirm cohere with each other. In our inductive pursuit of truth, there are techniques for gathering evidence—whether in the laboratory experiment or at a crime scene—to guide us into drawing logical conclusions from sufficient data. The multiplicity of truths uncovered through inductive processes of reasoning may or may not cohere with each other or with truths uncovered through our deductive reasoning processes. Often, specific incoherencies in our knowledge of things are temporary; new discoveries prompting new theories can wipe away old inconsistencies. Even so, it is always an unknown whether our experience of incoherency at any given point is due to the insufficiency of our knowledge or to an incoherent element in the nature of things. There are five large ways along which the Christian can proceed in relating faith to reason: the way of opposition, the way of harmony, the way of hierarchical order, the way of dialectical tension, and the way of mutual transformation.

1. The Way of Opposition

Here, reason has no authority in the realm of faith. The truths of religion lie beyond the bounds of reason. Rational processes, both inductive and deductive, are therefore irrelevant to the gaining of religious knowledge. Their use can lead only to false belief or unbelief. This view maintains that the so-called proofs of God are not, in fact, proofs of reason. They presuppose faith. Without faith, no one ever would have conceived the proofs. Further, reason can easily critique the arguments for God and even disprove the existence of God (philosophers have done both of these). Also, the God who emerges from the proofs—the unmoved mover, the ground of order and purpose, the highest being the mind can imagine, the necessary presupposition of our moral action—is a far cry from the loving, judging, forgiving, involved, responsive God revealed in Scripture. The criteria of reason (inner coherence, lack of contradiction, etc.) are human criteria and are not to be brought into judgment upon God's revelation in Scripture—or even upon tradition and religious experience when the church grants authority to these two. At best, then, reason plays no positive role in leading us to faith. At worst, it is destructive of faith.

2. The Way of Harmony

Here, reason and faith work hand in hand, seeking to discover the ultimate truths of God and existence. On the one hand, reason places bounds on the excesses of the religious imagination. Religious assertions are deemed false when they are logically contradictory or clearly defy those statements we know to be true through the scientific disciplines (especially the hard sciences of physics, biology, chemistry, and astronomy, but also of history, archaeology, sociology, and psychology). Religious people thinking in this mode would not say the world was created in six days, that Eve was created out of Adam's rib, that the Red Sea parted, that Jesus was born of a virgin, or that Jesus walked on water. On the other hand, reason when it is rooted in deep human experience—what Kant calls practical reason and what others call existential reason—leads us to affirm a spiritual reality. When reason reflects on the ultimate questions of life, it reaches toward belief in God and some form of eternal life to make (practical, rational, existential) sense of our longing for meaning, moral worth, and significance. Religion is the human search for that reality which constitutes the all-inclusive and ultimate truth of things. Reason keeps that search on target. Reason does not create religious practices, beliefs, symbols, and stories, but it allows us to interpret their true, inner meaning.

3. The Way of Hierarchical Order

Here, the relation between faith and reason is harmonious, but in a clearly defined hierarchical way. There is continuity from a lower level of rational religious truths to a higher level of revealed truth. Reason needs the truths of faith to complete its own pursuit of religious knowledge. The existence of God can be rationally established, as can the perfection of God's knowledge, power, and goodness. Through reason, we can understand ourselves as social beings with moral responsibilities. We can see that such qualities as courage, justice, loyalty, and peace are values to be pursued. But reason provides only partial knowledge of God, human nature, and human destiny. Full knowledge of spiritual reality lies beyond the capacities of reason. It is through divine revelation alone that we can know of God's triune nature, of the extent of God's mercy, of God's going out to us redemptively in Jesus Christ, and of the sending of the Holy Spirit to guide the faithful toward eternal life. Only through revealed truth do we learn of our true status as sinners, and that the highest virtues are faith in the goodness of God, love toward our neighbor, and hope for our eternal glory.

4. The Way of Dialectical Tension

Here, there is both an affirmation and negation of reason. It is not simply that reason has limits, which it does, but that it can be destructive of faith. Reason is always under suspicion, never quite to be trusted, even when it is being used in the service of faith, because it turns so easily toward sinful purposes and encourages the sin of pride. Having said this, reason properly understood can be affirmed as serving the interests of faith. Reason can lead us to the threshold of faith. It does so by raising questions about ultimate meaning—questions whose answers are a matter of life and death to us— and then showing us the futility of our attempts to answer them on our own. Reason drives us to ask whether there is any purpose to our existence or whether we are simply accidents of a creative but blind and senseless cosmic process; whether there is life beyond death or whether we simply return to the nothingness out of which we came. Reason can argue on both sides of these questions, and those similar to them, because it can always critique and negate its own affirmations. Our recognition of reason's inherent incapacity to provide secure grounds for faith can lead us toward atheism or agnosticism or it can become the occasion for genuine faith. When we acknowledge that we cannot achieve faith in God out of our own rational resources, then we can open ourselves to the God revealed in Scripture who alone can meet our ultimate needs.

5. The Way of Mutual Transformation

Here, as in the "dialectical tension" category, there is both a yes and a no to reason—though with a difference. Reason remains a source of corruption, but it is also an instrument for good, even for creative transformation. It is not so much that reason itself is corrupt as that corrupt or sinful selves reason, thereby introducing an element of sin into rational processes and results. We use reason to justify ourselves before God and our neighbor, to deceive ourselves as to the depth of our sin, to image God in ways that serve our own ends. On the other hand, the modes of reason, inductive and deductive, contribute in an ongoing, dynamic (never final) way to the human inquiry into knowledge of self and God. For example, our ever-growing scientific understanding of the development of life, and of the size and nature of the cosmos, provides us with clues into the way of God's creativity and the vastness of God's creative powers. Reason alone does not bring us to faith; it is more that, for the religious person, faith and reason interact so that each modifies and feeds the other. People of faith, using reason, are never through unpacking the meaning of faith's originating documents (scriptures) and interpreting and critiquing the church's historical dogmas. Faith and reason, then, have an ongoing history: Together they create a trajectory of understanding, or understandings. Reason, an ambiguous tool of faith, can lead religious people into new errors and new forms of sin, but also into greater depths of understanding and being.

Theistic Worldviews: Five Types

A worldview is a series of beliefs—sometimes stated conceptually, sometimes implicit in a narrative form—about the origin and nature of reality. A worldview provides a framework to answer the fundamental questions arising from existence: what is the origin of life? what is our purpose? our destiny? why is there suffering? why is there evil? what is real? what is illusion? In ancient times, we can find worldviews embedded in the myths of the Egyptians, Babylonians, and Greeks; in the creation and fall stories of the Israelites; in the dualistic metaphysic of Plato; in gnostic stories of the soul's descent into the physical world; in the Stoic philosophy of classical Rome; in the Hindu view of reincarnation and ultimate release; and in the Buddhist conception of no-self and the path to Nirvana. Modern times have produced new worldviews: the progressive view of history and the ultimate rule of reason that we associate with the philosophers of the Enlightenment; a nihilistic worldview combined with a will to power that found its full expression in Nietzsche's philosophy; Marx's view of history as driven by economics, conflict, and exploitation until a final revolution by the oppressed leads to an egalitarian society; and a secular view of the universe, finding life's origins in chance, its driving force in adaptation for survival, and its ultimate destiny in nothingness.

Christianity sits amidst these competing worldviews, respectful of some, antagonistic to others. Its worldview is (mono)theistic, as is Judaism's and Islam's. A theistic worldview shapes our answers to the fundamental questions through its conception of God's nature and power, and the way it understands God's relation to and activity in the world. In the history of the church, three types of theism have appeared, all claiming biblical ground: omnipotent theism, supernaturalistic theism, and relational theism. Two others have also appeared in Western thought: pantheism and natural theism (deism, Kantianism). In the main, the church has judged these latter unacceptable—too much at variance with the personal, active God witnessed to in Scripture. They are included here partly for purposes of comparison, partly because there are Christians who hold to them.

In all theistic worldviews, reality consists of God and the world; the differences among the five theisms lie in the mode and character of the God-world relationship.

1. Omnipotent Theism

God's reality is absolute transcendence. This means that God is a sheerly independent being, self-derived, complete, and perfect. God simply is what God is, in bliss and without change from eternity. God's "godness," so to speak, is this independence and the power it entails. God has no need to enter into relations with any other reality but is free to do so (from eternity). Indeed, God has the power to will anything into being. Of course, in the Christian tradition, God is love, and therefore only wills what is consonant with love (or, in Barth's significant revision, God freely wills to love—so not even love is a limit on God's freedom). In contrast, the world is completely dependent upon God for its origin and its sustenance. God can exist in perfection without the world, but the world cannot exist for one moment without God. God graciously creates the world with its own powers. But those powers neither limit God nor function apart from God's will. Nothing can happen in the world outside of the divine will. The world remains in God's hand. This does not mean worldly creatures have no will; but what we will, even when we will with all our heart and soul, God has already willed for us to will. Even when our will intends only to serve ourselves and is heedless of the welfare of others, God uses the negative consequences of our ill-will for an ultimately greater good. In this worldview, then, God is absolutely sovereign: the omni-active, providentially caring, all determining, ever-present power lying behind the world's determinations. Those who hold this view rest assured that nothing occurs outside God's loving will. No matter how senseless, how horrific, things may look to us, there are no chance events, no random happenings, no senseless occurrences. Of course, much happens that our minds cannot understand. The limitedness and sinfulness of the mind are a given. Also, there is mystery at the depth of things, not to be disclosed until the end, which lies entirely in the hands of an all-wise, loving, gracious, just, and merciful God.

2. Supernaturalistic Theism

This view modifies omnipotent theism in this way: Instead of thinking of God as immediately related to every worldly event—as the primary cause of every secondary cause in the creation—it thinks in terms of two provisionally independent realities, the supernatural and the natural. Each of these realities has its own order, its own laws. The prefix *super* indicates the higher, sovereign reality. The modification arises in part from the impact of modern science on our understanding of the natural causes of things. It also arises from the intensity of the modern concern for free will.

God remains an absolutely transcendent being with unlimited powers. But allowances are made for human freedom and a systemic understanding of cause and effect in the natural world. God, of course, has created the natural world, but that world is self-operating. It has its own order, it follows its own laws—the laws of physics, gravity, mass, light, energy; the laws of biology, genetic inheritance, generativity; the laws of chemistry; and so forth. God has put the laws of nature in place and permits them to operate on their own. God also creates human life with the capacity for free will. Human freedom, though limited, is real, both in relation to natural causation and to divine power. For example, in respect to nature, we are sexual beings, yet we can choose to lead a celibate, maritally faithful, or promiscuous life; we have an inherent craving for food, yet we can choose to fast for long periods, even to death. In respect to God, we are created to worship God and live in love and justice toward our neighbor. Yet we can choose to ignore our creator and to violate God's moral and spiritual commands. Not with impunity, however. The creation may operate under the laws of nature and human freedom, but it does so only by the grace of God. God can at any time break into the world, interfering with the laws of nature and overriding human freedom. Miracles arise out of this supernatural breakthrough into the natural. On the other hand, evil and suffering arise from a combination of natural cause and effect and the negative consequences of free will. God permits terrible things to happen partly for pedagogical reasons, partly for the maturing of our spirit, partly to assure that we come freely to faith. Even so, God remains in control of the ultimate outcome of things: the end of the creation, the end of history, our own end in eternal bliss or eternal punishment.

3. Pantheism

This view thinks not of two realities but of one reality with two dimensions: the order of things and the individual things themselves. The "things" are the particulars of our experience, the concrete realities: the tree growing in our backyard, the baby in the crib, the neighbor cutting grass, the plane flying overhead. All these seemingly disparate particulars are part of a great interrelated web, a network of connections grounded in the order of things. God is the order, complete and perfect, the eternal and unchanging ground of the passage of things. This passage is the concrete and moving expression of the order, so that divinity is to be conceived as the immanence of the world. God is related to the world as the dance is to the dancer. They are not to be thought apart. Reality is like the dance and the dancer; it is both form and act. As the form of the dance suffuses the dancer, so God suffuses the world. For the religious person who has this view, the world is drenched in God. All that happens is the expression of God; what is, is God's will. Ultimately all is one, and that one is God. The realization of this brings peace to the human spirit. It is the real content of salvation.

4. Relational Theism

There is God and the world, separate realities but inextricably related to each other. God is the eternal creator: the ground of the order, drive, novelty, purposiveness, and concreteness of the world. The world is the creation, dependent upon God for its ongoingness. Even so, the world is relatively independent of divine power; there is an element of self-determination or freedom in every creature's action as it responds not only to its own worldly environment but to the meaning and possibility that God places before it. There is then give and take between God and the world. God calls each creature at each moment of its life toward an action that maximizes its own and the world's well-being. The creature responds with its relative freedom to the relevant possibility that God laid before it—not simply yes or no, but more or less. God then responds to the creature's response, and so on. God transcends the world in that no creaturely activity can threaten God's eternal reality or alter God's character, integrity, or creative powers. God is immanent in the world in that God's aims for each creature are given to that creature in each moment of its existence. The world is also immanent in God, in that God experiences, "feels," takes account of, remembers, each creaturely action. In this sense, and in this sense only, Charles Hartshorne's phrase, "the world is the body of God," can be an appropriate metaphor for the God-world relation. God knows the world with the kind of immediacy that the self knows in experiencing heat on its fingertips, an image on its retina, sound through its ear, pain in the gut. Those who hold this view can rest assured that God never withdraws from the world. Quite the opposite. God knows, feels, the world as it is, in its joys and in its suffering, caring for us no matter what, always presenting to us possible courses of action that work toward our own wider good and the good of the whole. The suffering and evil in the world come from a combination of our finitude and sinfulness. Our hope to overcome evil in this world lies in God's patience and power to lead us to creative and healing possibilities that lie well beyond our powers of conception.

5. Natural Theism

God is the creator of the world. The order and design of the universe is the mark of the creator in the creation, the way an engine is the mark of an engineer, a painting is the mark of an artist, or a garden is the mark of a gardener. The creation, however, is self-sustaining. God has created a living world that operates as a closed system—requiring no further sustaining activities of the creator. Still, there is much evil in the world, brought about by the processes of nature and history. Moral obligation is part of the very order of being. This is particularly true for human beings, who not only can conceptually grasp the physical order of the world and the creator who lies behind it, but who are grasped by the moral order of being and the moral imperatives of the God who lies behind it. Human beings through conscience, experience, and reason can distinguish good from evil, and they realize themselves in freely choosing the moral life. Even so, the rewards of the moral life, in terms of recognition and happiness, do not necessarily lie in this life. In many cases, the moral life can end tragically or seem to come to nothing. This suggests an afterlife in which the moral receive their due reward. This suggestion comes to us not through a revelatory act of God but from our own reasoning capacities. The truths of religion remain within the bounds of reason.

Chapter 2

Doctrines

We turn now to doctrine—that is, to consciously held theological ideas. We need to be looking for tensions, even inconsistencies, between our doctrinal ideas and our hidden determinants. For practical purposes, we limit our analysis to five areas that trouble many of us in today's church: the problem of evil, the meaning of the (atoning) death of Christ, the relation of the church to the world, the relation of Christianity to other religions, and the interpretation of history and eternal life.

Theodicy: The Justification of God in Light of the Presence of Evil

The problem of evil is peculiarly sharp in Christian faith for this reason: We affirm that God alone has created the world and that the creation is good. We also affirm that, through no fault of God, the creation has fallen into disorder and distortion. Mythically speaking, we attribute the creation's fall—into the mix of good and evil, sin, suffering, and painful death that we know so well—to a freely willed, sinful act of the first human beings. Questions arise. How does a sinful will arise in a good creature? Could not God have created us so that we would only choose to realize good possibilities? And what are we to make of all those destructive natural events—everything from hurricanes devastating our homes to cancer cells devastating our bodies—where no sinful or evil intending agent is present? Could God not have created a more stable world of nature, a world without destructive upheaval? Further, there is the problem of the suffering of the innocent, particularly of infants and children; and the problem of senseless pain, not only in humans but in the lonely suffering of a wild animal. Why does God not prevent unmerited suffering or stop evil forces before they accomplish their great destruction? Christian theodicy seeks to answer these questions and others like them. Its purpose is to justify God as sheer love, power, and justice despite the long history of human horrors and natural disasters. There have been many theodicies in the history of biblical faith. They range in form from the dialogically suggestive book of Job written at least 2,500 years ago to the tightly argued, popular theodicy of C. S. Lewis and the more academic ones of John Hick and David Griffin.

Christian theodicies fall into three basic models. Each model differs in terms of its understanding of God's power and human freedom. Taking our clue from the nature and use of God's power, we can call these models unlimited dominion, self-limited dominion, and limited dominion.

1. The Model of Unlimited Dominion

This model dominates the theological tradition. It presupposes God's absolute power and freedom. That is where the "godness" of God lies. Power is the ability to determine what is. To be God is to be in control. Therefore, God can do anything and God determines everything. Whatever God wills is what happens; and nothing happens outside of the divine will. Of course, in this model as in all Christian models, God is more than power and freedom. God is love, justice, mercy, goodness, and wisdom. God is also omnipresent and eternal. Still, it is argued that these attributes, apart from absolute power, would not, philosophically speaking, yield us God but a finite, limited being; and would not, pastorally speaking, yield us a deity worthy of worship—for even a God of sheer love, who lacks absolute power, could not assure us of our redemption.

How does evil come into a world created and controlled by a loving and just God? Because freedom is a good, God allows for an exception to the divine control of things. God grants the first man and woman the freedom to sin or remain faithful to God. They abuse their freedom, and in so doing lose it, for themselves and for humanity as a whole. They bring sin into the world and, with it, suffering and death, not only for all human beings but for the whole creation. Henceforth, all human thoughts and actions are tainted with sin. It is no longer possible for us not to sin. Still, we are held accountable for our deeds—for though we are not free not to sin, we willingly commit sinful actions. All of us deserve to be condemned to eternal death. If God were only a just God, that would be our fate. But God is also a God of love and has resources of mercy that transcend the demands of justice. From eternity, God has foreseen our sinfulness and has provided for us: Jesus Christ will come and will die for us that we might have salvation.

Terrible events and the suffering they cause are explained as God's just retribution for our sinful ways, as the means by which God moves us toward moral and spiritual maturity, or as a testing of our faith. Even so, not all suffering can be rationally accounted for. Some sufferings are so great, so out of proportion to our individual sins, that neither divine retribution nor any other explanation seems sufficient. Mystery remains in God's creation. Some things are hidden from us. Our minds are too finite, our concerns are too small; we cannot see the whole picture, nor can we see to the end of time. Even so, through faith, given to us by divine grace, we continue to believe that God is love and that everything has a good purpose. In the end, from the perspective of eternal life, God's loving providence in all things will become clear to us, even those things that now appear to us as surds and as mere wreckage.

2. The Model of Self-Limited Dominion

Here, God's power is unlimited in principle, but (self-) limited in fact. God could control the actions of all creatures but instead places a voluntary and provisional limit on divine power so that creatures may freely exercise power in their own right. God permits us to be free. The reasons for this are several. A world in which humans have free will is a greater and more glorious creation than one composed of beings inwardly programmed or supernaturally willed to do only good. Also, there is no shortcut to becoming a fully mature self, one capable of profoundly loving God. Maturity, "soul-making," can occur only through a developmental process that presupposes the freedom of the will, temporal passage, and learning through experience. Abstract reasoning, book knowledge, and the wisdom of an oral tradition are not enough. We need to make errors of our own choosing, to take responsibility for our actions, and to learn from them by living with their positive and negative consequences. Finally, God takes more pleasure in love and worship freely given than in love and worship that spring from the necessity of one's nature.

Evil is real. It is not mere appearance. It is the price we pay for the greatness of freedom and the nature of the maturing process. Even so, there are evils that neither contribute to the maturing process nor seem worth the price of freedom. Not all suffering can be justified as pedagogically useful or necessary to God's ultimate plan. In this view, God could intervene to prevent such evils and unjustifiable sufferings but, appropriately, does not. Here are the reasons. If God mercifully intervenes in one place, there is no logical place to draw the line for God not to mercifully intervene in other places (the slippery slope argument). Once we know of God's past interventions and anticipate God's future interventions, the world will lose its consequential character. The sense of an order of things, so necessary to the development of the healing arts and sciences, will be absent. Further, those times where God refuses to intervene will appear arbitrary to us, even unjust. Selective divine intervention, then, would worsen the theodicy problem rather than resolve it. It would inhibit the soul-making process—by encouraging resentment and waiting for God to take care of problems—rather than strengthen it.

The full justification of God, then, must await the end. From the viewpoint of eternal life, and from looking at the whole history of creation and salvation, we will come to agree that the great end of the salvation process, the making of souls that freely and joyfully love God, infinitely outweighs the genuine suffering brought in its wake.

3. The Model of Limited Dominion

Here, the theodicy issue is resolved by allowing love to inform the definition of God's power. This leads to a qualification of or limit upon divine power. The argument goes this way: Love respects the freedom of the other; therefore, divine power can no longer be defined as the ability to determine what is. Without that definition, the question "Why does God permit evil?" does not arise, and the problem of God's power overriding human freedom is avoided. Instead, God's power in relation to the world is defined in terms of persuasion, direction, and influence. Because it is God's power we are talking about, that power is maximal, universally present, and necessary. No earthly entity, from the merest cloud puff to the most complex creature, can have its being apart from God's power; God is the ground of order, meaning, purpose, value. God's power lures the world toward increasing creativity and heightened well-being. But in an interdependent, relational world, God, though the one necessary reality, is still only one among the many realities that bear down upon us and affect our being. There are other powers in the world, powers of nature, history, and culture—the land on which we live, the nation, the ethnic group, the family, to mention only a few. We respect and sometimes give allegiance to these powers, rightfully so, but they can draw us to values and actions in conflict with God's intentions and purposes. Evil comes into the world not simply because we stubbornly, bullheadedly resist God's will, but also because the "goods" we pursue, the values that attract us, are often in conflict with each other. Loyalty to one's nation and social group may come into conflict with loyalty to family or to justice to the stranger or alien. Similarly, freedom comes into conflict with equality; the pursuit of beauty can come into tension with the pursuit of justice; and truthtelling can conflict with love. Our world is one of conflicting values, moral ambiguities, and inevitable tragedies. In this world, God is ever present, drawing us toward the best possible outcome representing the good of the whole. The "best possible" may often involve suffering and destruction. God works within the limits of the possible, though of course the possible at any given time may well be beyond our current assumptions and even imaginings. God does everything that can be done to prevent suffering and evil; still, the limits are real, and, in any event, outcomes remain partly dependent upon the response of the creature to God's lure toward new possibility.

There is no final justification of all evils and sufferings. Some horrors are sheer wreckage. They lack all justification. It is only by the grace of God that, even so, we affirm the essential goodness and worth of the creation—and give thanks for our participation in it.

The Atonement: The Meaning of Christ's Death

Reinhold Niebuhr described the atonement as "the significant content of the incarnation." He meant that the clue to Jesus' being lies in his redemptive work. Christ's death sits at the center of his work. We ask ourselves: Why does Christ have to die? What is the saving significance of his death? How can the death of one person atone for the sins of all? Why is redemption tied to suffering? The doctrine of atonement seeks to answer questions of salvation arising from Christ's death.

Jesus dies on the cross. The gospels tell us he was betrayed by a disciple, arrested by the Jewish authorities, and sentenced to death on the cross by the Roman governor. We are so used to this story that we miss its original shock. Jesus' followers hope he is the Messiah, God's agent to usher in the long-looked-for kingdom of God, a time of great glory, a time for God's will to be "done on earth as it is in heaven." Instead Jesus is crucified, and the world goes on in its usual ways. Christ's followers flee Jerusalem, dismayed and fearful for their own lives. They expected a new age, not the crucifixion, an ignominious and scandalous way of dying. How could this one be the promised Messiah, the Christ? Jesus' death, then, is at first seen as a sign of failure. That is how matters lie until his followers experience the risen Christ. The resurrection appearances convince them that Jesus is, after all, the Messiah. As Niebuhr noted, the Messiah that came was not the Messiah that was expected. That is, Jesus did not fulfill the tradition's idea of the work of the Messiah. The church saw that the work of the Messiah must be understood differently. This new understanding starts with what Christ has, in fact, done. He has brought into being a new community who know him as their lord and savior. There is a new age, but it is not the age of the kingdom but the age of the church, a time for mission and evangelization. The age of the kingdom is deferred to a second coming of Christ. Further, the new community now affirms Jesus' death as the divinely intended mode of our redemption. He died, "according to the Scriptures," that we might be saved. The reference here is primarily to the suffering servant passages in Isaiah 53—though the New Testament provides a variety of positive images and concepts relating to Christ's death. Christ is a propitiation for our sins, he gives his life as a ransom for many, he is obedient unto death, he is a sacrificial lamb, his blood is the blood of the new covenant. These images have produced a number of ways of understanding the redemptive or atoning meaning of the death of Christ.

Over seventy years ago, Gustaf Aulén, in a widely accepted study, distinguished three main types of the idea of the atonement in the history of the church's thought.[1] He entitled these types the Christus Victor theory, the satisfaction or substitution theory, and the exemplar theory. To those three, we can add two recent types: the existential theory and the relational theory.

1. The Christus Victor Theory

There are two ruling notions here. First, human salvation is an objective event accomplished by divine power. It involves God, Christ, and the devil. Second, human sin has (rightly) put us under the power of death and demonic, destructive forces.

This theory uses mythical imagery to express the rationally inexpressible: our captivity to negative powers and our absolute dependence upon an act of God in Christ for our liberation from them. Our salvation occurs through a cosmic drama, played out by God, Christ, and the devil. Because we have sinned, turning from God and abusing our freedom, God gives us over to the devil, to the powers of sin and death. Human existence is now caught in a vicious circle from which it cannot emerge. The more we sin, the more powerful and prevalent is sin's hold upon us. Thus, the devil comes to have rights over us. The devil, of course, is the enemy of God, a metaphysical other, insofar as he represents the forces of evil. Paradoxically he is also the arm of God's judgment upon a sinful world. The devil's rights cannot be disposed of arbitrarily. This means sin and death cannot be overcome simply by divine fiat. The devil, who represents the power of negation, must in some way rightly lose his power over us. So Christ, the Son and agent of God, becomes the bait of redemption. Christ offers himself on the cross to the devil as a ransom for humanity. The devil accepts the bait of Christ, releasing humanity from his power, but then cannot hold Christ because he had no right to hold the innocent One. Mythically, the devil has been tricked by God; metaphysically, evil overreaches itself in trying to contain the good. The negative lives off the positive, which it distorts and undermines, but it cannot completely overcome the positive (the Son of God) or it would destroy itself.

The atonement, then, is the divine action in Jesus Christ, a once-for-all cosmic, objective event, which breaks the power of the devil and liberates us from the conditions of bondage. There is no rationally coherent way to express this action, but the meaning is clear. In Christ's death, God has destroyed the power that destroys us. That is gospel, good news, to be proclaimed to humanity. The power of this theory lies in liberating us from our fears that we have lost our lives to powers of destruction. We can live our lives now with the certainty that, no matter what happens, eternal life is our destiny.

2. The Satisfaction or Substitution Theory

The two ruling notions here are first, that human sin creates a tension in God between justice and mercy; and second, that human salvation is an objective event, accomplished by God and Christ. Christ takes the punishment we deserve, so that God's mercy can prevail without violating God's justice.

This theory uses the courtroom, its legal terminology, and the notion of penance as the explanatory metaphors of the atonement. We all participate, knowingly and unknowingly, in human sin. Therefore, all of us stand guilty before God. Our just desert is eternal condemnation. God, however, is not simply just; God is also merciful. But how can God be just and yet merciful to us? The answer lies in the substitutional penance of one who is both fully divine and fully human. As fully divine, Christ is sheer perfection, without blemish; as fully human, Christ is capable of suffering and death. The suffering and death of one who is sheer perfection is of infinite worth—a more than adequate expiation for the infinite weight of human sin. God's justice is satisfied. God can now act mercifully—and forgive us of our sins. They no longer count against us. Objectively, we are redeemed.

The theory is legalistic, quantitatively weighing sin and suffering, but its power is psychological. It gives full play to the depth of guilt in the human psyche and to our feeling that justice requires punishment for our sins. The mere declaration of God's forgiveness or even of God's defeat of the devil would not remove our guilt-consciousness. Forgiveness without justice is sentimentality; it does nothing to break the actual force that holds us in bondage: our own sense that, corporately and individually, we have violated justice and must pay the price. In Christ's death, one who represents us pays the price; indeed, the price Christ pays has infinitely more value than the cost of our sins. Justice, then, is given its due. Christ's death for our sins has the power to release us from the bondage of guilt and self-condemnation—even though we remain in sin. We are, simultaneously, sinner and saved.

3. The Exemplar Theory

The two ruling notions here are first, that the life of self-surrendering love is at the center of Christian faith; and second, that Christ models that love and inspires us to live likewise.

This theory stresses the importance of human participation in the processes of redemption. For that reason it has been labeled subjective, though it contains the objective element of the life of Christ. Atonement here is not a once-for-all cosmological event accomplished for us by God in Christ, but an ongoing event that takes place again and again each time Christ's life of love arouses a believer to live similarly. In Christ we see revealed the fullness of human life. Here is the way God intended human life to be. For God is love, and love is what God wants from us. Christ is the great teacher, the role model for all of us. His commandments show us what we can do and be. His sufferings are divine instruction about love. His power lies in his capacity to persuade. His teaching and exemplary life awaken in us what is deepest and truest, empowering us to live as he lived. Insofar as we live a life of love for others—ministering to those in need, working for greater justice for others—we are realizing life in the kingdom, living the redeemed life.

The great strength of this theory lies in its understanding of God as love, of the Christian life as a life of love, and of our active participation in the atoning process. It affirms that, in God, love and mercy, not wrath, are ultimate. It recognizes that even in sin we remain free to respond to Christ's call, and that we bear responsibility for what we make of our lives, whether for salvation or destruction. Its weakness, which is the other side of its strength, lies in its failure to take sufficient cognizance of the power of sin. It is silent on the hold sin has on us despite our best efforts. It ignores the cost of our past sins to others and ourselves. It overlooks the ways that the consequences of sin linger on well past the initial sinful act, destructively intruding on our lives and those of others even as we seek to put our sinful ways behind us.

4. The Existential Theory

The principle of participation plays the dominant role in this theory, working in two directions. From God's direction, our salvation involves God's participation in the suffering of the world. From our direction, salvation involves our participation in the processes of atonement initiated by God.

Christ is the central manifestation of the power of God's being in finite existence. It is not the only manifestation, but (from the Christian perspective) it is the central one, and the criterion for all others. The cross signifies the subjection of Christ, the incarnate one, the mediator of God, to the destructive consequences of sin (estrangement or alienation from God, self, and others).

It is the sign that our sin is costly, not only to us but to God. The suffering of Christ manifests the suffering of God. On the cross, God experiences, takes in, the sufferings of the world in order to redeem them. Christians, therefore, looking at the cross of Christ see not simply the suffering of a man from Nazareth but God's atoning activity in and through suffering.

The resurrection signifies the victory of Christ over the destructive consequences of existence. It is the manifestation of the power of divine being over all that is destructive to finite being. In God's life, all that is negative in existence is taken in, overcome, and transformed. God suffers in order to overcome suffering. That is the atoning activity of God. When we participate in the suffering and resurrection of Christ, we participate in a power grounded in Being (the most general term for God), which eternally overcomes the power of death and estrangement. That is the atoning activity of God. The suffering of God, as manifested in Christ, is neither a substitute for our suffering nor a metaphysical accomplishment of salvation apart from our freely willed activity. We realize salvation not through theoretical knowledge of God's participation in the suffering of the world but through existential knowledge. Salvation involves freely opening ourselves to God's suffering, participating in it, being transformed by it. In so doing, we become a new creature, reborn, so to speak. Though our lives remain riddled with ambiguity and the anxiety of guilt, and though we only fragmentarily realize our "new" being, still we live with participatory knowledge that nothing, ultimately, can separate us from the love of God.

5. The Relational Theory

There are three ruling notions here. First, sin is separation, loveless division, our refusal to recognize our belongingness to each other; second, the atonement is God's action in Christ working toward reconciling us to each other and restoring us to the community of love; third, God is relational, maximally so: To be God is not only to affect all others, it is to be affected by all others.

In the teaching and suffering of Jesus, we see one who remains loyal to us even in the face of betrayal, denial, and rejection. The suffering of Christ signifies not the price exacted by God for our forgiveness, but the spirit of love and forgiveness bearing with us even at great cost. That spirit is God's spirit, so that Christians see in Christ the steadfast, suffering love of God. God suffers because suffering is a consequence, a cost, of loving those who live in violation of their essential belongingness to each other. God's forgiveness does not overlook violation; it takes the pain of violation into itself. Further, God's suffering signifies not only the cost of our sinfulness but the extent of God's love and care for us. God loves us even unto suffering for us. In suffering with our suffering, feeling our feelings, God communicates to us the depth of the divine love for us. In knowing that God feels the depth of our suffering as we feel it, we experience the healing love of God.

Christ's suffering, then, has transformative power because it reveals the costly and participatory character of God's love for us. But there is a second, social, dimension to God's atoning activity. The life of Christ creates a new community, the church, which takes its origin and definition from the spirit of love that the disciples knew in Jesus and that the church now experiences in its own midst. This new community, grasped by God's forgiveness, understands itself as living in the power of a spirit to overcome divisiveness in our lives and in the lives of others. The church, then, is not so much a consequence of the atonement as its continuation. It knows itself as a community whose work is the reconciliation of life to life. Christian existence is life in a community that lives by faith and participation in the ongoing atoning action of God in Jesus Christ. Wherever the power of a loyal and forgiving spirit overcomes the broken relations of individuals and communities, there the church sees the atoning action of God known through Jesus Christ.

The Church and the World: Ethics and Ecclesiology

How do our beliefs as Christians, and our membership in a church community, inform the stance we take on the social and moral issues of our time? There is no simple answer to this question. Individual Christians, and the churches to which we belong, hold widely divergent views on a variety of issues. That does not mean any view espoused by a church or a believer is as valid as another. We are back to the difference between pluralism and relativism: The fact that a number of views are valid does not mean all views are valid. But why would Christian ethics be pluralist rather than absolutist? Why can the churches not speak with one voice on public issues? Surely that would be politically more effective and provide clearer direction to Christians looking to the church for guidance. Why isn't there just *a* Christian stance on, for example, abortion, stem cell research, the death penalty, divorce, war, homosexuality, and so on? Odd as it sounds, there are good theological reasons for our lack of unanimity, for our not coming up with a single "right" and final view on so many issues.

There is, first, the biblical understanding that we are creatures, finite in all respects. Accordingly, there are limits to individual and communal knowing. In any given situation, we cannot know all the factors present, we cannot see all the possible consequences of an action, we cannot understand from within all the perspectives involved. We draw our conclusions from partial knowledge and from differing perspectives—no wonder we come up with different understandings and, over time, as our knowledge and perspective change, these understandings change. We are not, after all, God; we neither see things from God's all-inclusive point of view nor know all the possible consequences of our decisions.

In the second place, there is the biblical understanding of sin, which extends to both individuals and communities. Human beings are sinful; even our best judgments and actions contain elements of sin. The problem is not simply that we do not know the good, but we resist knowing the good, sometimes consciously, sometimes unconsciously. And even the good we know, we may resist doing. Our pride in self, so important for our psychological health, can distort our thinking; our concern for self can distort our values; our capacity for self-deception can blind us to the truth. Group pride, the pride of belonging to a particular community, can be even more blinding and destructive in its consequences than individual pride—because it involves mass influence and corporate power. Sin, then, qualifies our moral judgments in many different ways, leading us to differ widely on ethical issues. Even when we put ourselves on guard against the problematic dynamics of our finitude and sinfulness, we cannot escape fully from them—though we sometimes try to convince ourselves that we do.

There is yet another reason for our pluralist ethics, identified by H. Richard Niebuhr more than fifty years ago.[2] Niebuhr noted that no one is simply a Christian, that no one simply takes their identity, their ways of seeing and being, from Jesus Christ. All Christians find themselves in a culture that provides them with a language, a community that cares for and educates them, an economy that produces and distributes food and other necessary goods, a legal system that provides social stability and order, and a history that traces their cultural origins and shapes their character. For this reason, Christians find themselves with a cultural identity and a religious identity, a dependence on culture and a dependence on Christ, a loyalty to their culture, and a loyalty to Jesus Christ. Christians, therefore, have to answer a question, consciously or unconsciously, regarding their culture. How are they to reconcile their loyalty to Christ and Christ's cause with their loyalty to culture and its values? Niebuhr discovered that in the history of the church, there were five large ways, all with biblical grounds, in which Christians answered that question. Each way of answering leads to a type of Christian ethic that is at variance with the others in certain key respects. Niebuhr categorized the five types as: Christ against Culture (that is, against the values of the culture),

Christ of Culture, Christ above Culture, Christ and Culture in Paradox, and Christ as Transformer of Culture. All the types have their strengths and weaknesses. Each of us will find that some are weaker than others, though we may differ on which these are. This typology is still useful, but it is not necessary to repeat it here. It might be more pertinent to our preaching today, given the current emphasis on communal identity and the ecclesial character of faith and ethics, to transpose Niebuhr's Christ and culture typology into a church and world typology. Doing so will allow us to uncover the connection between our ethical thinking and our understanding of the nature of the church. The way we conceive the church, particularly in its relation to the world, leads to different ways of understanding the Christian ethic, and the way we think about Christian ethics leads to different conceptions of the church. Understanding these relational dynamics and their variety should prove helpful to our preaching on social issues and faith identity. Here, then, are the typological categories: the church against the world, leading to an ethics of opposition; the church with the world, leading to an ethics of harmony; the church above the world, leading to an ethics of hierarchy; the church and world in paradox, leading to a dualist ethics; and the church as transformer of the world, leading to an ethics of conversion and relativity. To exemplify the distinctiveness of the categories, there will be a discussion of each type's perspective on war and violence.

1. The Church against the World: The Ethics of Opposition

Here the church is imaged as a community of holy people called out from the world and its sinful ways, empowered by the Holy Spirit, and living in obedience to the commandments of Christ. Jesus is the law-giver. The fact that he gives a command means we have the capacity to realize it. Those commandments are found in the Sermon on the Mount, the gospel parables (the good Samaritan, the last judgment), the gospel stories (the rich young ruler, the woman caught in adultery), and so forth. In living a life guided by the commandments, members of the community experience the inner peace of life in God's kingdom. Informing every aspect of this life is the refusal to engage in or sanction violence, even in the face of evil.

The world, in this view, signifies both socio-political structures and institutions and the way of being (mode of existence, set of values) implicit in these structures. The world is the great tempter to a false and idolatrous way of life; it lures us with its promises of power, prestige, status, money, material comfort, and amusements; it turns us against our neighbor, encourages us to put our own needs ahead of all others, and leads us to forget that we are going to die. The world, in sum, draws us away from what really matters, which is that we should love and care for each other and put our faith in God's promise of eternal life. Most condemning of all, the structures of the world—the political, legal, and economic institutions; the tax systems and property rights; the courts, prisons, and even schools—are sustained by the state's readiness to use its own legalized forms of coercion and violence (the police and the military). Even in times of (seeming) peace, the world exists by (implicit) violence.

The church unmasks the sinful foundation of the world, withdrawing from its structures of violence. She thinks of herself as a holy people, not participating in the sin of the world. Withdrawal allows her to avoid sanctifying state violence and minimizes the corrupting influences of the world's values on her. In spiritual intent, the withdrawal of the community is absolute. In practice, absolute withdrawal is not possible, and there is room in this view for a range of understanding regarding the degree of withdrawal. On the far end of that range is the withdrawal from society's structures into relatively self-sustaining economic communities with little involvement in the political and social life of the wider culture. On the other end is the willingness to participate in the nonviolent professions of the world (everything from medicine and teaching to carpentry and logging) and even in the political process. (This is the difference, broadly speaking, between the Amish and Mennonite communities.) The withdrawal in the latter case is from participation in and responsibility for the coercive and violent forms of power that sustain the social and political structures. But it is not (at least, not necessarily) a withdrawal from publicly critiquing the values of the wider society and the policies of the state. This is particularly true on the issue of war and peace.

The church unconditionally rejects warfare as an instrument of foreign policy. It does this because Christ forbids us to do violence to others. We are to avoid evil; violence is an evil, and nothing can make it a good. There can therefore be no talk of justifying warfare with a "national self-defense" or an "ends justify the means" argument, as if a good consequence can make an evil act (killing another) anything other than evil. All churches of this type will refuse to participate in or support a nation's war effort. Members of these churches will go to jail or accept alternative forms of service rather than take up arms. Some members will refuse to pay taxes during a time of war, on the grounds that they cannot allow their money to support state violence. Others will show their opposition to war through the political process (writing to congress, the president, and so on) and by public demonstrations—though this type of church would never countenance resorting to violence as a means of opposition.

2. The Church with the World: The Ethics of Harmony

In this category the church is imaged as the teleological agent of God. God calls the church into being as the means to fulfill the moral-religious purpose of the creation. That purpose is the (gradual) realization of God's kingdom on earth, a time when all human life will exemplify the values of love, justice, respect of others, freedom of conscience, social cooperation, and peace. Jesus is the founder of the church, the inspirer of her mission, the preacher of the coming kingdom, and the teacher of its values.

The world, in this view, signifies civilization—the human attempt, through the development of knowledge, to turn the powers of nature to humane purpose. Nature's destructive powers are the basic human problem. Humans are concerned about justice, suffering, peace; nature seems indifferent, even hostile, to our concerns. Droughts cause starvation; floods and volcanic eruptions create havoc; disease destroys life indiscriminately. Through science and technology, we gain control over the negative forces of nature. We create machines to mass-produce goods and automate labor, discover drugs to cure diseases, use fertilizers and irrigation systems to multiply the food supply, devise transportation and communication systems that extend to remote corners of the earth, and so forth. Of course, we do not necessarily use the powers of the civilized world to good purposes, nor do we know, let alone pursue, the true goods of existence. For a variety of reasons—ignorance, insecurity, long-standing hatred between groups, demeaning social environments—we use the powers of technology to exploit and destroy each other, adding the horrors of history to the ills of nature.

The church is the bearer of the true values of human existence and the true end or aim of civilization. There is an essential (though not yet actual) harmony between the kingdom of God and the civilization of the world. In principle, the church provides the values of life and the world provides the technological powers for their realization. In fact, of course, there is conflict. Civilization develops social structures and values that work against the values of the kingdom. The church, therefore, must function as the prophet and evangelizer of the world. As prophet, she condemns the world's false values and unmasks the socioeconomic systems and policies that engender those values. As evangelizer, she works both to convert sinners and to inspire the converted to become social reformers.

The dynamic energy of the church comes through Jesus. He inspires us as the model of what we all should and, ultimately, can be; and by forgiving our sins he helps us overcome the despair and paralyzing guilt of our ethical failure. Through this energy, we increasingly inject the values of the kingdom into the structures and policies of the world. As social reform occurs, the causes of human sin begin to be eliminated. The world gradually progresses toward the kingdom—and in so doing moves toward its own fulfillment.

In this view, warfare, like our other sinful ways of relating to each other, belongs to the long and painful process of our historical development. The church preaches and works for peace, but it knows well that wars and other forms of violence will not be eliminated until the social conditions that breed violence are eliminated. On the one hand, then, there are social grounds that account for war and even, on occasion, make it unavoidable. On the other hand, the church's mission is the progressive elimination of those grounds— and her long-run expectation is peace on earth.

3. The Church above the World: The Ethics of Hierarchy

Here the church is imaged as a divinely established institution providing sacraments and structures for the completion and fulfillment of all human life. The church has a two-fold role: to penetrate the whole of society with its religious-moral values and to prepare the faithful for eternal life. The key principle in its doing so is hierarchy. Within itself, the church allows for a plurality of levels of religious authority and modes of existence (secular, priestly, monastic); and it conceives of its relation to the world as a higher order affirming and transcending a lower order.

The world, in this view, signifies nature and society, both of which are grounded in God. God has established the laws of nature and the (political, economic, and other) orders of society. Humans participate in both nature and society, so we are subject to the laws of both, and in that subjection (with some exceptions) we are obedient to God. Our capacity to reason is part of our nature and provides us with the means to uncover the natural laws of the physical and moral universe. There are natural virtues—justice, self-control, courage, and so on—that reason can recognize and humans can achieve. We are social beings by nature, with the capacity and the need to organize ourselves politically and economically. We create the arts—music, painting, sculpture, theatre, literature; all these are legitimate and valued parts of the life of the world.

The church relates harmoniously but hierarchically to the powers and achievements of the world. The church, for example, recognizes that human reason can know God as the "unmoved mover" or "ground of order," and then adds the knowledge that can come only through revelation: the triune nature of God, the redemptive power of the cross of Christ, and so on. In a similar way, the church sees the natural virtues as providing only an incomplete happiness; full happiness depends on living out the supernatural virtues of faith, hope, and love. Although the church legitimates the structures of society, including political parties, armies, police, law courts, and prisons, it works to infuse religious-moral values into all social institutions and actions. Business activities, for example, are limited by the principle of fair price; the acquisition of property is allowed, but not simply for selfish ends; wars between nations are accepted, but only within the stated limits of just war theory; political rule is legitimate, but not tyranny; medical research and practice are limited by the principles of natural law.

The church organizes itself hierarchically both to establish lines of authority—so that the church speaks with one voice on doctrinal and ethical matters—and to resolve the problem of the impractical character of Jesus' radical commands. No business could maintain itself if its income were distributed to the poor rather than to its owners and workers. Similarly, politicians could not function responsibly if they felt compelled to sacrifice the interests of their own country in favor of the interests of the enemy. Law courts would produce social chaos if judges and juries felt compelled to forgive all who came before them—nor could police apprehend criminals if they renounced all use of force. The church, therefore, finds these activities legitimate and necessary, and yet she knows that obedience to the commands of Jesus constitutes the highest form of human existence. To resolve this contradiction, the church thinks in terms of stages of holiness—from the ordinary Christian life of politicians, police, and business entrepreneurs, to the eucharistic and pastoral life of the priest, to the holy life of poverty and prayer of the monastic—and for each stage provides appropriate structures of existence with a corresponding ethic.

On the issue of war, the church's hierarchical structure allows for two positions. On the one hand, the church can in certain cases legitimate the wars of a nation and the participation of Christians in those wars. On the other hand, for those called to obedience to the radical commands of Jesus, the church's clerical and monastic orders allow for a life of nonviolence.

4. The Church and World in Paradox: The Ethics of Dualism

In this category the church is imaged as a community of faith where the gospel is preached and the sacraments are celebrated. The faithful are simultaneously saint and sinner. Sainthood refers to the spiritual state of faith: our accepting the gospel that Christ dies for us, forgiving our sins and granting us salvation. Yet, the "saint" remains a sinner, in will and in act. The reason is the presence of evil in human life, even among the good and the faithful. We remain, therefore, throughout our life, ever dependent on and grateful for God's forgiveness through Christ. This inner sense of gratitude for the undeserved mercy and love of God is central to the life and worship of the church.

The world, in this view, signifies the spirit and structures of society. These structures are necessary for human existence. We need governments with the authority to make and enforce laws; we need economic and financial systems (with their promise of profits) to insure an adequate production and flow of goods; we need armies to protect us against external threats, and police to secure us within our own borders. But these structures, for all the good they allow, are grounded in negativity. They presuppose and seek to restrain our aggressive, violent, deceitful, selfish—in a word, sinful—nature. Without socially imposed restraints, including coercive ones, life would be anarchic and brutal; with them, there can be order and even a measure of justice. For that reason, God ordains the social structures—everything from the forms of government to the class structure in society, to the courts and prisons, to the armed services. On the one hand, the existence of these structures assumes the prevalence and power of sin; on the other hand, they are seen as coming from God for our sustenance.

The church affirms God's presence both in its own fellowship and in the life of the world. But the modes of that presence are radically, even paradoxically, different. In the worship of the church and the inner life of the Christian, God is present as our loving, merciful Lord, forgiving all our sins, calling us to forgive others, to give unselfishly to those in need, to not resist evil, to do no violence, to not judge others, to refrain from taking a neighbor to court, to live in meekness and humility. In knowing God's love and mercy, we gain intimations of life in God's kingdom; a sense of grace and forgiveness; a freedom from guilt, anxiety, and doubt. On the other hand, God is present in the world as the Lord and judge of history, turning a wrathful face upon us for the ways we afflict and oppress each other. God calls those who bear responsibility for maintaining the order of the world to use our worldly powers to restrain the anarchic, destructive powers of sin.

Christians, therefore, live with two ethics: an ethic appropriate for their life in the world of sin, and an ethic appropriate for their life in the fellowship of Christ. Luther used to say that we live in two kingdoms (a problematic though useful metaphor); the key in taking action is to know which kingdom we are in at any given time. The Christian functioning as judge in a law court draws upon an ethic appropriate for the kingdom of the world, where sin must be restrained. In this kingdom, God calls upon judges to exercise retributive justice: Criminals must be punished proportionate to their crime. On the other hand, in their personal life, in the kingdom of God, a judge is to respond as Christ would to an injury suffered from another. When a judge forgives a friend for an act of personal betrayal, he or she rightly is drawing upon the ethic of God's kingdom.

In this view, wars are a horrible but not a surprising phenomenon in the kingdom of the world. As Lord of history, God calls us to take up arms where necessary to put down the violence that otherwise would increase the state of injustice, destroy the civil order, and, perhaps, threaten the existence of the church. Even so, killing remains a sin, for which we are to ask God's forgiveness.

5. The Church as Transformer of the World: The Ethics of Conversion

Here the church is a community of people hearing God's judgment upon themselves and their world and responding to God's call for change. The word of judgment reveals the true state of our affairs: We have corrupted our human nature, directing it to the wrong ends, living divisively, and creating divisive social structures. The fault is ours; it lies in the self's consenting to, and even willing, its own corruption. But the church also lives under God's redemptive powers, which awaken her to new possibilities in self and in the world—for these powers are at one with those by which God created the whole of things. Redemption, then, draws the church not away from the wider life and doings of God's creation but deeper into them—with the intent of transformation. Even so, the church knows that despite her intent, her actions can never fully escape from the context of sin and betrayal that marks all of human life.

In this view, *world* encompasses the whole of existence: the world of nature and the world of history. Both nature and history are understood dynamically. Each is seen in continuity with a past order, yet ever changing and open to the new. The historical sphere includes the laws, institutions, and customs of society. These serve, at least in part, as a bulwark against human evil and sin. Prisons, law courts, and police forces are only the most manifest instruments of deterrence that society provides. More subtle forms are spread throughout society—in the home, the work place, and the schools. Even so, these aspects of society are also seen as instruments for the good. Our economic, social, and political systems can draw out from us unexpected gifts and talents, provide us with creative work, affirm us in our respect for self and others, and build up our life together so that we can live in relative peace and justice with one another.

The church confesses God as the creator: the ground of the world's dynamic being. The key to the world's dynamism lies in the God-given elements of freedom and inner determination, good in themselves and yet entry points for sin, so that although the world is inseparable from God there is never an identity between God's will and the world's realizations. Despite the sin, the moral and spiritual ambiguity that cuts through the whole of existence, the church affirms that this world remains God's creation and that Christ reigns over life. The creative powers and goodness of life (which the church knows as Christ) are deeper than the powers of hate, death, and destruction—and these two are in battle. The kingdom is an embattled kingdom. History is the battleground where God and people grapple with human sin and with the moral and spiritual corruption of the good creation. History is where the forms of sin are manifested but also where they can be overcome. There can be real achievement in history; the forms of sin, such as slavery, ethnic hatreds, and sexism, can be defeated. But there can also be loss. There are no guarantees, and new sins can always arise out of the corruption of the all-too-imaginative human mind. The fullness of God's kingdom, therefore, always lies beyond history, and yet we do not come into that fullness apart from history.

Wars are terrible. They can be justified only where the consequences of avoiding a war are judged more evil than the evil of war itself. Such a tragic situation can arise because of the presence of radical evil in human life. Our own evil brings the horror of war upon us. Nations and peoples can become driven by the desire to exploit, dominate, and even destroy other peoples and nations. In dealing with such a situation, there are no sinless options. Sometimes the only option is chaff. Where this is the case, God can call us to war. There is agreement with the dualist view here. It differs from dualism in holding out the hope that we can create institutions and laws that help ward off the kinds of conditions that make wars inescapable.

The Relation of Christianity to Other Religions

There is a history, sometimes a violent one, of Christianity's relation to other religious traditions. The church, from its beginning, entered into conflict with other religions that were in many places incompatible with Christian faith and whose adherents refused to acknowledge salvation through Christ's death on the cross. The church today deplores the use of violence in the furtherance of her faith or any other faith—and, on the whole, she worries about appearing exclusivistic in her relation to other religions. Still, the church remains evangelistic, marked by the mission to bring the gospel to unbelievers. Some argue that the church is essentially mission: always going out from herself to others, witnessing in word and deed to Christ her Lord. There is little quarrel with this understanding (at least within Christianity) when mission is defined as ministering to the social and psychological needs of the poor, the victims of injustice, the sufferers from abuse. But there is little agreement, and some confusion, when the church turns to her mission to evangelize. In today's globalized world, where different faith communities sit side by side, even the definition of the *unbeliever* is an issue. Is the unbeliever the one who lacks faith in salvation through Christ—so that the world divides into Christians and unbelievers? Or is the unbeliever the secularist, the one who adheres to no religious tradition and who denies the reality of any dimension transcendent to the physical world—so that the world divides into believers (among whom are the Christians, Muslims, Hindus, Buddhists, Jews, and others) and secularists? In this case, do all religions provide valid, though differentiated, pathways to salvation, or are the other religions in some ways spiritually unequal to Christianity, lacking certain of her truths, upholding false beliefs and false ways of being? If the former, should the church seek to convert only ex-Christians, urging other unbelievers to return to the faith of their original heritage? How the church answers these questions informs her way of relating to other religions and their adherents. It not only affects her mode of mission but has political and sociological consequences as well. In some ways, these are old questions in new forms. Ancient Israel struggled to understand her relation to the other nations, providing a range of answers from Isaiah's universalistic "light to all the nations" to Ezra's exclusivistic focus on the Jewish people. The early church, as Paul's writings suggest, was particularly concerned with the relation of Christianity to Judaism, its parent. This relation, still an uneasy one, contains problems peculiar to it and requires its own distinct typology.

The relation of Christianity to the other religions breaks down into five types: radical exclusivism, the way of rejection; radical inclusivism, the way of identity; hierarchical pluralism, the way of stages; radical pluralism, the way of otherness; and dynamic pluralism, the way of mutual transformation. The relation to Judaism breaks down into three types: supersessionism, eschatological mysticism, and forked parallelism.

1. Radical Exclusivism: The Way of Rejection

Here Christianity makes an absolute distinction between its own origin and the origin of the other religions. Christianity originates in divine revelation, attested to in the Scriptures of ancient Israel and the early church; the religions originate in the power of human needs and the human imagination—God being an idea projected upon reality to satisfy our need for love, security, meaning, purpose, and order. Further, in this view, salvation comes from God alone. There can therefore be only one true salvation history: that of ancient Israel culminating in the life, death, and resurrection of Christ and the coming of the church in the power of the Spirit. The other religions reflect attempts at self-salvation through human striving to reach God. Such attempts are doomed to failure, for the human mind is finite and sinful. Our finitude limits the scope of our thinking, so we cannot truly conceive a (divine) reality wholly other from ourselves; and the conceptions we do arrive at are distorted by our sinful tendency to have them reflect our own interests.

This view takes a completely negative approach to the validity of other religions, rejecting all their claims to truth. It does so on the basis that no point of contact exists between God and (sinful) human existence; that is, we lack both innate knowledge of God and the capacity to experience God. Out of love, God elects Israel as a vehicle of revelation and a preparation for Jesus Christ. Now, through Christ, God can be known and salvation preached to all peoples. The church has the mission of bringing the gospel to all. In doing so, she may enter into dialogue with people of other faiths, partly to show loving concern for where people are, but ultimately for the purpose of conversion.

The harder version of this view connects salvation to the proclamation and acceptance of the gospel: Only those who know the truth can be saved. Here, the distinction is between the saved (Christian) and the unsaved other. The softer view, drawing forth the implications of Christ dying for all, allows for salvation outside of Christian faith. Here the distinction is between the Christian who knows and rejoices in salvation and the other who lacks this knowledge and joy.

2. Radical Inclusivism: The Way of Identity

This type affirms the oneness of all religions in their essence. The differences we see in religions are peripheral to their essential truths, which we discover by looking for what they have in common and by noting resemblances even amidst their differences. We are to look, for example, at the way all religions affirm an ultimate reality; call us to recognize and relate to it; provide us a purpose for existence; establish forms of worship and meditation in order to open us to transformation; lead us to pursue such ethically visionary ideals as justice, peace, and compassionate love; and sustain us with hope for an ultimate happiness.

This view, then, validates all religions, though not the truth of all religious claims. It assumes that all peoples have the capacity to experience and reflect upon the ultimate or transcendent dimension of reality, and that the religions represent the organized human response to that salvific experience. The conflicts among the religions arise from the different particulars of their history and culture and the peculiar genius of each religion's founder and its later leaders. The truths of religion can be derived through a process of abstraction from the particulars of religious practices and beliefs. These truths, generalizations held in common by all the religions, do not constitute another religion. They are a philosophic overview of all the actual religions. Dialogue seeks this philosophic overview, in the hope that it may lead the different religions toward reconciling their conflicting claims and the hostilities that resulted from them. Even where such reconciliation occurs, the religions retain a peripheral distinctness—differing in forms of worship, details of practice, and accent of thought and belief.

3. Hierarchical Pluralism: The Way of Stages

Here Christianity distinguishes herself from other religions in terms of higher and lower, complete and incomplete. Christianity is the highest religion on the basis of the fullness and finality of revelation in Jesus Christ. All religions contain some element of truth, even the most primitive, though the scope of truth can vary greatly from religion to religion. There is thus an ascending order of religions according to the degree of their truth (and falsity). The scriptural witness to God, itself completed in the revelation in Christ, provides the norms for determining the relative standing of each religion.

On the one hand, this view affirms the religious life in all its forms as a sign that all humans have some sense of God and of their need for salvation. This knowledge can be accounted for on the basis of the notion of general revelation and the human capacity to experience and think about the transcendent. On the other hand, except for Christianity, all religions are viewed as incomplete and even misleading in their understanding of God and salvation. The fullness of God's truth, which is the essential desire of all peoples and all religions, lies through Christ alone. Christianity then both connects with and completes the other religions.

The church respects all religions on the grounds that all have partial knowledge of God and that people of every faith have a relation to God. Though the church has a clear mission to evangelize—to bring the fullness of God's truth and redemptive power to all peoples—she also seeks to understand the nature of other religions in order to discover the specific points of connection to Christian faith. The church enters into dialogue with the immediate purpose of gaining understanding and the longer-term purpose of conversion.

4. Radical Pluralism: The Way of Otherness

Here Christianity calls attention not simply to its own particularity and otherness, but to the particularity and otherness of all religions. Religions are irremediably foreign to each other, each religion having worked out its relation to God through its own peculiar history, culture, and language. It is a mistake to think that the essence of a religion lies under its particulars, as if peeling away the particulars will uncover some general ideas we then might compare with the general ideas underlying other religions. Rather, religion takes its identity from its particulars, especially its dominant ones. When we change these particulars—such as specific linguistic terminology, symbols, or doctrines—we are striking at the identity of a religion. For example, Christianity confesses God as Father, Son, and Holy Spirit, and celebrates the sacramental presence of Christ's body and blood in the eucharistic bread and wine. These words and symbolic objects are not expendable expressions of some deep philosophic truth but are themselves the truths of the Christian community. The case is similar with the language and sacred objects of other religions. The differences among the religions are real and permanent. Any attempt to reconcile the conflicting claims of the world's religions is misguided, based on a misunderstanding of the nature of religions.

Religions should be likened to games such as baseball, chess, bridge, and monopoly. We do not arrive at the truths of these games by looking for notions common to all of them. And if we revise a game's rules and practices so that it looks more like another, then we lose the game itself. Nor can we understand a game—say, chess—by thinking of it in terms of the rules of another game—say, baseball. We understand a game by learning its rules and playing it. Then we know and live out its truths, so to speak. The same is true of religion. We must learn its language and doctrines, and participate in its practice—and then we shall know its truths.

In this view, Christianity is complete, particularistic, and confessional. Christ is its internal norm—not some general principle used to evaluate the truth of other religions. Those religions have their own beliefs and practices, which from their inside constitute their truths. This is a radically pluralistic view, ruling out any possibility of a philosophic overview. A strictly hard-line approach would see dialogue as futile—those for whom the rules and practice of baseball are the complete truth of things cannot understand chess movements. But dialogue is possible in a softer view—those who love baseball and find it fully satisfying can get some understanding and even appreciation of chess by listening to and watching its practitioners. Dialogue, then, would be for the sake of mutual understanding, a way of showing respect and promoting a peaceful tolerance among disparate groups. Evangelism would take a form appropriate to radical pluralism: the openness of the Christian community to all people who, for whatever reason, find themselves attracted to the Christian life.

5. Dynamic Pluralism: The Way of Mutual Transformation

In this type, Christianity affirms both its otherness from and its openness to all religious traditions. For this position, it is as true to say that Christianity's distinctness from other religions is permanent, as that Christianity is open to transformation from other religions. It is also as true to say that salvation lies through the life and person of Christ, as that the religions are a sign of the omnipresence of God's creative and salvific power.

Christianity begins with a particular event or series of events: the life and teachings, the death and resurrection, of Jesus Christ. God's revelatory presence and full redemptive activity is here, in these particular words and these particular acts, and in this particular time and place. In this particularity lies Christianity's dynamism. To lose it is to lose itself. But this view also gives weight to the Johannine affirmation of Jesus as "the Word made flesh." The eternal Word of God, who was with God in the beginning and through whom all life is created and sustained, is the same Word made flesh in Jesus Christ. Here this view finds the basis not only for Christianity's claim to universality but for a creative encounter between Christianity and other religions. God's Word, which we know in Jesus Christ, is the same Word that empowers the life and faith of all peoples. Many factors account for the rise and spread of the many religions, but the sine qua non is the givenness of God's power and presence in all life. Even so, there are real differences among the religions, not only because people see God through their particular culture, history, and language but because God's presence is always particular to its context. God is not present to us in a general way—that notion is a conceptual abstraction, not a datum from a living faith—but always as a specific response relevant to the particular limits, needs, and possibilities of a situation. Thus Christianity cannot understand other religions through some general theory but only by listening to a faith's self-interpretation, that is, through dialogue. Dialogue begins for the sake of mutual understanding and then becomes the occasion for mutual transformation. We are led to rethink our beliefs, and perhaps modify them, in light of insights from other religions. Transformation leads a faith deeper into its identity rather than threatening its particularity. The religious situation remains pluralistic and dynamic: differentiation and change, manyness and metanoia, are permanent. For its part, Christianity is never through unpacking the meaning of Christ's life, death, and resurrection—and the insights that come through dialogue with other religious traditions are but another means to that end. Here, religion is not likened to a game that takes its identity from rules exclusive to itself. It is more like a living organism, relational, responsive, and growing—its identity continually forming itself out of its particularity of origin, the trajectory of its history, and a certain consistency of character. Part of Christianity's consistency of character is its openness to all people, its faith that in its own particular forms of worship, God's redemptive powers are available to all. Evangelism walks the fine line between inviting searching individuals into the worship of the church and respecting the validity of all the world religions.

Excursus: The Relation of Christianity to Judaism

There are three ways that Christianity interprets its relation to Judaism.

1. Supersessionism

Here the church replaces Israel as God's elect people. Christ's coming both reveals and fulfills the true purpose of Israel. Israel, like a John the Baptist writ large, "prepares the way for the Lord." Her long history constitutes the initial stage of God's plan for the salvation of humanity through Jesus Christ. The sacred writings of Israel can now be truly interpreted as pointing to and containing the promise of Christ. These writings, now named the Old Testament, find their completion in the New Testament—which witnesses to the life, death, and resurrection of Christ and the emergence of the new community in the power of the Holy Spirit.

In principle, Israel should recognize Jesus as the long-expected Messiah. The fact that only a relatively low percentage of Jews did so presents the church with a theological puzzle and a missionary task. In resolving the puzzle, supersessionism divides into a hard and soft line. The harder line takes the way of rejection: The faith of Israel has exhausted its meaning and purpose; it has lost its valid spiritual ground and should wither away. That it has not is due to stubborn pride, particularly strong in a people who do not want to give up their elect status. Therefore, Judaism can only be viewed as a field for mission; dialogue can only be for the purpose of conversion. The softer line takes the way of stages. Judaism is like the other religions: She has some understanding of God and the life of faith but lacks the fullness of the revelation in Christ. Judaism can therefore be accorded the respect and relative validity that Christianity grants to all other religions. Dialogue can be for the sake of mutual understanding, though the impulse to mission remains as a strong motivating factor.

2. Eschatological Mysticism

Here the Jewish faith and people remain within God's plan of salvation. Though the Messiah has come, God is not yet through with Israel. She has one last mission, an eschatological one, which will become clear only at the end. Therefore she remains an elect people alongside the church, serving a purpose unknown in its details and perhaps even unacknowledged by herself.

The church, for its part, grants Judaism full respect. She sees Israel's refusal to accept Christ as due not to sin but to God's providential will. In the end, at the eschaton, there will be a joyous coming together of the two faiths. Then, all knees will bow to Christ.

3. Forked Parallelism

Here Christianity and Judaism are viewed as two branches off the same trunk, separate though related religions, each valid and authentic in its own right. Both emerged in the first century (the fork in the road) from the religion of ancient Israel—a religion centered in Jerusalem, practicing a sacrificial form of worship at the temple, presided over by an official priestly caste, and with a tradition of prophets arising from time to time out of the people. What we call Judaism is Rabbinic Judaism with its center in the local synagogue, its rituals in the home, its leadership in the learned rabbis, and its written authority in the Hebrew Scriptures (especially the Torah), the Talmud, and the long tradition of biblical commentary.

The two religions share the authority of their common source: the faith, history, and sacred writings of ancient Israel. They branch off from each other in stressing and developing different elements in those writings. Christianity, centered in Jesus Christ as the fulfillment of Israel's messianic expectation, draws out the universalism already present in ancient Israel's faith. The very nature of the gospel, that Christ died for all people, gives Christianity a sense of mission that propels the church outward. In proclaiming the gospel to all the nations, Jews and gentiles, the church is led to revise the notion of the elect to include any person who acknowledges salvation through Christ. For its part, (Rabbinic) Judaism, responding to the destruction of the temple, the Roman expulsion of the Jews from Palestine (the promised land), and the Christianization of the Roman Empire, stresses the particularistic elements in the notion of election. The Jews remain God's elect people, chosen for a specific purpose: to keep the law of Moses contained in the Torah and to hear the word of the prophets.[3] What Judaism loses in universalism, it gains back in intensity of religious identification.

A variant of this view, taking its cue from radical pluralism, refrains from any attempt to define Judaism, insisting that religions can only be known and should only be defined from within. Those taking this view, while acknowledging substantive differences between the two religions, believe it an error to encourage any invidious comparisons. They prefer to emphasize the depth of Jewish theological writings and the profound spiritual life displayed by so many of her practitioners. Both of these views are open to dialogue for purposes of mutual understanding and goodwill.

Endings

"In my beginning is my end." The words are T. S. Eliot's. He is trying to move us into thinking existentially, and then religiously, about death and its effect on meaning. He does so by playing on the double meaning of *end*. First, *end* means finish, termination, final status. This birth body, which is mine, which is me, is mortal. Because I begin as a mortal, I will come to an end, I will die. This horrifies us; it seems so unfair. We find ourselves with such a strong will to be that not-being strikes us as an absurdity, an anomaly, and such a painful one that it is almost unthinkable—and yet it never lies far from our thoughts. "To be or not to be," trite though it sounds because it's so often quoted, is nevertheless one of the great human questions, and every religion deals with it—each in its own way. The Christian response, that Christ died that we might have life eternal, lies at the heart of our faith's confession. And so Eliot, the believer, can turn his words around. "In my end," he writes, "is my (eternal) beginning."

End also means aim, purpose, intention, meaning. And so, following Eliot again, we can say, "In the beginning is my meaning." But that begs the question, for it leaves unanswered the content of my meaning. So I find myself with questions. Why did I begin? For what purpose? Why did life begin? To what end? How can I know the meaning of my beginning before I know my end? These are not merely academic questions. We want meaning in our lives; we want to see some point to our existence. The absence of meaning may not strike us at first as being as horrifying as the loss of life, and yet those of us who find our lives meaningless also find that we are drained of our will to live. Death takes away our life, but so, ultimately, does meaninglessness. In fact, the two are intertwined. Death not only threatens life physically, it threatens everything that gives life meaning. Everything that I value, that I live for—my children, my work, honor, fame—all seem good and worthwhile, but they can pass away at any time. Someday it will be as if they never were. What's more, nothing that was had to be. What, then, was their point to begin with? The historian says that everything participates in history, that we all contribute to history. But what is history? Does history have a point, a meaningful end, or is it just a bottomless pit, a black hole, a darkness into which everything falls?

Christianity affirms the significance of history, in that God's revelatory, liberating, saving power breaks into the history of a people. In faith, we say the way to know God is to listen to Israel's and the early church's witness to God's activities in their midst. In the exodus from Egypt, God liberates a people from slavery; through the words of the prophets, God demands justice; and in the life, death, and resurrection of Christ, God is reconciling the world. History, then, is the arena of God's revelatory and redemptive activities—which the church is to proclaim to all people. History is also the locus of God's transformational purposes, for God calls us into the ways of love and justice. Thus our historical activity finds its ground of meaning in God. In faith, the temporal looks to the eternal for its significance. It is not odd then that in Christian usage, the kingdom of God bears both a trans-historical and an inner-historical sense. Depending on context, it can symbolize life beyond temporal-historical existence (the kingdom above) and/or the participation of the eternal in the temporal-historical (the kingdom is coming or the kingdom is within).

The theological interpretations of history and of eternal life raise related yet distinct issues, so that each requires its own typological set. The church thinks about the kingdom and the meaning of history in five large ways. We can call these ways other-worldly, apocalyptic eschatology, realized eschatology, dialectical, and evolutionary. There are three ways we categorize the church's thinking of eternal life: individualistic, communal, and mystical. In addition, there is a fourth way, a *via ignota,* which rests content with Paul's statement that "nothing can separate us from the love of God."

The Kingdom and the End (Aim) of History

There are five theological interpretations of the meaning of history.

1. Other-Worldly

Here, the kingdom of God lies above the world. In a particular time and place, in the life, death, and resurrection of Jesus Christ, God breaks into world history to redeem humanity from its bondage to sin and death. Prior to this action (from the call to Abraham to the birth of Jesus of Nazareth), history serves as the preparatory ground for Christ. Following this action is the age of the church: History is where we hear the gospel and respond in faith or unfaith. In other words, history has meaning as the scene of God's salvific action. Nothing else is to be expected from it, other than the negative function of providing a proving ground for faith. The values of the world—wealth, power, fame—serve as temptations from faith in God alone. The afflictions of the world—pain, loss, death—serve to test the authenticity of our faith. There is an unbridgeable gap between the kingdom of God, above, and the kingdoms of the world, below. They do not, and never will, intersect. All our world-historical actions are tainted with sin. History runs on, but it has nowhere to run. The ambiguities of life remain unconquerable and cannot be purged from our existence. The world will always be a vale of tears; its history will always be turning into a butcher block. This view discredits all impulses to transform history, because they would prove futile. The most we can do is create small church communities of patient martyrs and pilgrims. Our lot is to live within history's ambiguities and terrors; our task is not to live by them. Instead we must keep our eyes on the forthcoming prize of eternal life in another world, in God's heavenly kingdom.

2. Apocalyptic Eschatology

In this way of thinking, the kingdom of God lies before us; it is coming soon—and suddenly. History runs toward a catastrophic event, a time of disruption and suffering for all, but also a time of reckoning for the dark forces that have soiled, corrupted, and finally taken control of the kingdoms of the earth. There will be signs of the end, wars, disease, and then a great battle where God defeats all the anti-Godly powers, cosmic and earthly, demonic and political. History has come to its day of judgment: the "tares" shall be separated from the "wheat" and destroyed. Now the Messiah returns, ushering in a new era. God's kingdom will have come on earth.

In this view, the kingdom of God is not produced by any kind of historical development. It is independent of any historical situation or human activity. It arrives as a strictly unconditioned act of divine intervention. Even so, it represents, in a negative sense, a fulfillment of history. The demonic powers defeated by God are related to the political-historical powers of the period. Those who threw their (historical) lot in with the demonic forces receive eternal condemnation.

Finally, the new age, though temporal-historical, is an age of unambiguous life. The creation has a fresh start. Unlike the fresh start after Noah, God's will is now writ in our heart—and the cosmic-demonic powers that corrupted our will and ruled over our lives have been forever destroyed. Sin and death are no more. There is only joyous obedience to God's will.

3. Realized Eschatology

Here, the kingdom has come, inwardly and spiritually, and its blessings are available to those to whom it has been revealed. In Christ, God confronts us, showing us the way to fulfillment, asking us to walk in the way of the Spirit, calling us to decision, bringing upon us a life-crisis. For those who respond positively, there is pure joy, like the joy at a wedding feast, or the joy of a woman who discovers a lost coin, or the joy of a shepherd who finds the lost sheep. This joy comes not from some happy, sudden change in our fortunes, as if walking in the way of the Spirit leads to nothing but bright consequences. The kingdom is not utopia. It does not turn either an individual's history into utopia nor history at large. The joy of the believer is the joy of participating in the eternal. This is not an escape from history—for the believer finds the eternal through involvement in the forces and causes of history. History is valued as the vehicle of the eternal. Even so, meaning is not dependent on the achievement of historical goals, which are notorious for being compromised or unrealized or, even when partly achieved, for being ephemeral. Further, the participation of the believer in the eternal, in the kingdom of God, is not a once-and-for-all event. God confronts us with the decision to walk in the way of Christ throughout our lives, and our joy in responding to our last call is as fresh as to our first.

In this view, there are three key categories: the eternal, the temporal or historical, and the moment in which the eternal intersects the temporal-historical. The moment of intersection is the presence of the eternal in history, and the opportunity for us to participate in the kingdom. Christ is the pattern for the relation of the three categories; he is the Word made flesh, the eternal appearing in time. He remains present in power through the scriptural and proclaimed word, bringing us, in the moment of confrontation, to a time of judgment, calling us, again and again, to decision.

4. Dialectical

Here, the kingdom lies ahead, but it never arrives; also, it lies above us. What happens in history matters, both to God and to us. God calls us to work for peace and justice in the political and social realms. There is expectation for the transformation of social structures. Old evils, old injustices, can be overcome. Even so, sin remains; historical life does not lose its ambiguous character. The very process of overcoming old injustices can involve moral compromise and lead to new forms of injustice. No achievement, no matter how great, comes without the price of negativity. There is always God's "yes" and "no" to the achievements of history. Also, no achievement is invulnerable to loss. Therefore, though there can be real gains in history, history never fulfills itself. Complete fulfillment awaits eternal life.

This view stresses both the transcendent and the inner-historical sides of the kingdom of God. On the one hand, unambiguous life, complete fulfillment, can only lie beyond history. Faith in God's promise of life in a kingdom or community of perfect love is faith in the realm of eternal life. This faith in life beyond life helps us through the defeats, frustrations, and compromises of historical-political life. On the other hand, the kingdom of God participates in the dynamics of history. But it is an embattled kingdom, symbolizing God's power on earth struggling with the destructive forces present in groups, nations, and empires and their laws, customs, and institutions. God calls the church to participate in the embattled kingdom of God.

Jesus appears in the midst of the ambiguities of history to initiate the new community (the church), to reveal the meaning of history (participation in the embattled kingdom of God), and as the full manifestation of saving power (within and transcendent to history). Christ is God's saving power, incarnate and effective in the processes of history, working to change social structures and laws. Through Christ, history reveals its self-transcending character, striving toward an ultimate fulfillment that ever eludes it.

5. Evolutionary

In this view, the kingdom is coming slowly, progressively, with some setbacks but with an inexorable, long-term forward movement. The key analogy is between the development of biological life and the development of spiritual life. Life took millions of years to move from the earliest simple organic compounds to the complex forms of physical being we know today—with apparent dead ends along the way (a hundred million years of dinosaurs, for example). Nevertheless, life is marked by increasing physical complexity, leading to a qualitative leap to mental life. Now, in human history, we are witnessing the evolutionary trajectory of moral-spiritual life—also with setbacks as serious as the ones that plagued the evolutionary development of biological life.

The Spirit of God participates in both the dynamics of nature and history, drawing biological life into increasing complexity and mental life into increasing intensity and harmony. The kingdom is the telos of God's creation, its vital, driving force. It is also the full realization of God's creative intent and the perfect embodiment of creaturely life. Christ is the alpha and the omega, the beginning and the end. The world is created through Christ the Word, the Logos; and Christ, as we knew him in the flesh, is the image of the new creature at the end.

There are two variants of this view. The first conceives of the creation as never finished and thinks of human history as infinitely open to new and more perfect futures. Progress has no end; life continually drives on to greater intensities of love, deeper forms of communion, more complex harmonies of being. The kingdom of God always lies ahead. The second variant looks to fulfillment, to a final stage of history in which the ambiguities of life are conquered and the kingdom of God arrives on earth.

The Kingdom and Eternal Life

There are four ways of thinking about the nature of life beyond death.

1. The Individualistic View: A Vision of Many-ness

Here the emphasis is on the preservation and perfecting (where *perfecting* means completing) of the individual person or personality. A person is a center of consciousness and will; a subject of awareness; an agent of action; a unique, mutable, sometimes glorious, but always flawed being. Death marks the end of the ever-changing, imperfect states of temporal existence and the beginning of the eternal state of the person now brought to individualized perfection. In the kingdom of God, each individual, though one among many, is an autonomous personality, distinct, self-enclosed, standing in joyous relation to God and to others.

In temporal life, the person is an embodied self in space/time. Where the resurrected life is conceived physically—taking its cue from the gospel stories detailing Jesus' resurrection appearances—eternal life is conceived as God's perfected reconstruction of the physical body, and the kingdom of God is imaged as another, though transcendent, spatial environment. Where the resurrection is conceived spiritually—taking its cue from Paul's concept of a spiritual body ("it is sown a physical body, it is raised a spiritual body")—then physical embodiment is no longer conceived as necessary to personal, individualized existence, and the kingdom is thought of as a spiritual reality beyond space/time.

2. The Communal View: A Vision of the Many in the One

In this view, the notions of communion, participation, and relation inform the meaning of perfection and shape the character of life in the kingdom of God. Perfect life is life in communion. We become persons only through relationships, so that the perfection of the individual lies through the intensification of relationship. In the kingdom of God, the consciousness of the self becomes transparent to other selves; the self now feels not only its own feelings but the feelings of others. This notion opens the possibility of universal salvation through a purgatory-like experience. For example, the rapist, feeling the feelings of the person he had raped, would be moved to repentance, as would the Nazi upon feeling the anguish of the Holocaust victim. Similarly, groups involved in long histories of ethnic hatred and violent acts of vengeance, upon experiencing the feelings, hopes, and passions of their enemy, would find their own negative feelings transmuted—and would be moved to reconciliation. In knowing from the inside what it is like to be the victim, the perpetrator becomes open to transformation. On the other hand, the victim would experience the transformed feelings of the perpetrator. This mutual inclusivity of feelings would lead people into understanding, repentance, forgiveness, reconciliation, and, finally, joy—in other words, into a community of love. In this community, the many remain many, for each person is their own center; but the many also become one, for the personal centers live as a harmonious, interconnected whole.

In applying the notion of relation to our understanding of God, the kingdom of God can be conceived as lying within the life of God. In this view, all life contributes to the divine life and, ultimately, participates in it personally, so that the harmony of our eternal life is part of the eternal harmony of God. In the kingdom, then, we are not only at one with each other but at one with God. In such a state of harmony and total community, Paul's idea of a spiritual body rather than a physical body appears as the more felicitous notion. At a minimum, we can say that physical embodiment is not necessary in this view of eternal life.

3. The Mystical View: A Vision of Oneness

Here the aim of existence is to return to our ultimate identity with God. All life comes from God; the many (creatures) come from the (transcendent) One. In this view, God's oneness is interpreted as undifferentiated unity, so that eternal life, which is life in God, is life beyond differentiation. On the other hand, finite, temporal life is characterized by separation, differentiation, and complexity. Language, which reflects our experience of finite and differentiated existence, cannot adequately describe our experiences of God. We call our experiences of God *mystical* precisely because those experiences lie outside the boundary of what (finitely) is. What we experience, insofar as we can express it at all, is a oneness with God, an absorption into deity, a sense of loss of self, which is felt as ecstasy and interpreted as reality. This mystical experience provides both the clue to how to live now (lose concern for self, live selflessly) and to the nature of the afterlife. In the life to come, separation and differentiation are overcome; particularity and individuality are shed. In dying, we die to the self and to all that separates us from other selves and from God. In the end, we are at one with God, and God is all in all. In this view, the kingdom of God can be likened to a great sea. We are the raindrops, having risen from the sea, now falling back into the sea—and this, we know, will be paradise.

4. The Via Ignota[4]

In this view, we rest content with the faith that nothing, including death, can separate us from the love of God in Christ Jesus. We cannot say what it means for death not to be able to separate us from God. Our experience and imagination are too limited to provide us with anything but futile, even if interesting, speculations and visions. To have faith in God's love is sufficient for our life of faith now.

PART 2   How to Use the
          Theological Profile
          _____

Preliminary Remarks

*I*n part 2, we will suggest ways you can use the theological profile as a tool
to become more theologically intentional in your preaching. We envision the
theological profile being used as part of a class or workshop as well as for
week-to-week sermon work by individual preachers. Chapters 3 and 4, therefore, are filled with excerpts taken from a workshop in which the profiles were
used. These examples are provided to demonstrate some of the ways you can
use the profile in a small group or in your own sermon preparation. In chapter 5, we conclude part 2 with two of our own sermons accompanied by brief
commentary based on our own profiles.

We assume you, having read part 1, have begun to piece together your basic
theological profile. In order to achieve an overview of your theology, photo-
copy the Theological Profile Chart in appendix B of the book and check one
box in each category that best matches your theological commitments. Keep
this chart in front of you during sermon preparation, referring to it often. Let
it point you back to appendix A (The Theological Profile [Short Form]) and
to part 1 for more information whenever necessary.

When we teach a class or workshop for preachers, each participant makes
a copy of his or her Theological Profile Chart, distributing it to other participants to have on hand during the remainder of the class. In that way, the entire
group can refer to it as they brainstorm sermons together, or as they offer feed-
back on sermons preached. In chapters 3 and 4 you will see how this process
works.

In the process of sermon preparation, we ask for two basic sets of theological moments during which careful and intentional theological reflection takes place. The first set of theological moments occurs during sermon
brainstorming. As you sit with Bible open and with commentaries and

theological books in a convenient place, it is important to keep your theological profile within reach. At the intersection between the biblical text and life, you must constantly ask theological questions: "What is God doing here?" "What is the theological subject matter that is emerging, and how should it be shaped?" "What category in the profile is most relevant to my reflections?" "Is there further reading I need to do in order to deepen or expand my understanding of this topic?" "Am I letting the text guide my theological reflection?" "What am I avoiding theologically within this text?" "Why?" The process of arriving at something to preach should be filled with these kinds of theological questions. The theological profile will help you in this process.

In chapter 3, we highlight several of these theological moments, looking at some of the ways in which the profile can help you to ask theological questions, address theological issues, and maintain a consistent theological perspective during sermon brainstorming. We include excerpts taken from a workshop in which several preachers used the profiles during collaborative sermon brainstorming. Each of our preacher-participants shared their exegesis of a biblical text while we and the other participants helped them see ways their theological profile might help them to decide what to preach, and how to preach it.

Once you have decided on a theological message and purpose for a sermon, you do not leave theological reflection behind. As the larger message is parceled out piece by piece in the sermon, it is crucial that each portion of the overall message receive special theological attention. The next set of theological moments, therefore, occurs during each point, move, or sequence of sermon writing or preparation. Anytime you introduce a new or different thought in the writing of a sermon, you must take time out for theological reflection. "What am I saying at this point?" "What are the theological implications of what I am saying?" "What, within my theological profile, must be considered in order to give this thought theological depth and integrity?" If these and other questions are asked during the crafting of sermons, you will increase the theological consistency and coherence of your sermons.

Chapters 4 and 5 explore in more depth some of the ways theology informs the actual choice of language, logic, illustration, and sermon style. Chapter 4 highlights several theological moments that are crucial for sermon composition. Again, we have included excerpts of conversation, taken from the same workshop, that show some of the ways the profile can be used when writing sermons. In chapter 5, we each provide a sermon with a running commentary that accentuates the theology communicated in the language of the sermon.

By providing you with these chapters filled with excerpts and sermons, our goal is not to cover the profile, providing examples of each category in a sermon. Our group of preachers was not diverse enough, nor is there adequate space in this book, to explore every possible use for the profile. Instead, we want to show you some of the ways you can use the profile to help you begin to incorporate both of these sets of theological moments into sermon preparation. We also want you to see how the use of the profiles can inform and strengthen the critical reflections of a group of preachers who are learning how to make better use of their theology in preaching. It is hoped that, after reading these three chapters, you will learn more about the role of theology in sermon preparation and see how the theological profile can help you become more self-aware and intentional as a theologian in the pulpit.

Chapter 3

The Theological Profile and Sermon Brainstorming

The first set of theological moments we want you to consider in this book takes place in a variety of ways during the text-to-sermon brainstorming process. This chapter contains excerpts from our group of preachers as they engaged in lively conversations about biblical texts they were preparing to preach. These excerpts illustrate some of the ways the theological profile can be used in sermon brainstorming. Our goal was to make use of the theological profile of each preacher-participant to help them become more theologically aware and intentional when they work with biblical texts.

These excerpts in no way exhaust the many ways the profiles can enhance theological awareness as you reflect on the meaning of biblical texts. We have chosen a variety of excerpts from the group discussion by our preacher-participants that exemplify some of the more important roles played by the theological profile in sermon brainstorming. In the margins next to these excerpts of conversation we make brief comments that suggest some of the payoffs for using the theological profiles. When you finish this chapter, you should be able to see how the profile can help you add several significant theological moments into the process of exegeting and interpreting biblical texts for preaching.

Correlate the Biblical Text and Life

Use the profile to help you theologically correlate the biblical text and life. In our experience, it is common for preachers to err on either side of the text-life equation. Sometimes issues from the life side are imposed on the biblical text. This usually means preachers go in search of biblical proof-texts that are used to shore up a narrow theological, experiential, or cultural bias. If you tend to be a life-issues preacher, you have much to gain by raising theological questions of the biblical text that arise from the hard issues of life (suffering, divorce, racism, sexism, and so on). The problem, however, is that you may find yourself forcing the text out of its own theological galaxy into an orbit that only barely connects with your message. When this occurs, you have effectively short-circuited the theological wisdom that resides within the biblical text.

On the text side of this equation are preachers who spend most of their time traveling down every exegetical river or tributary in search of something to preach. If you are a text-centered preacher, you have much to gain by attending to the faithful theological testimony of our forebears in the faith. You may discover, however, that more often than not, your message fails to have any real relationship with the lives of your hearers. You may find yourself disregarding the theological issues arising from life today while you rehearse a set of biblical concepts and narratives that only marginally relate to today's world.

The best practice is to take a particular text and to bring it into a sustained back-and-forth theological conversation with ordinary life and the culture in which we live. In this process, you permit both the text and life to raise theological questions of one another. In our experience, *your theological profile can help you raise these questions and clarify their answers.*

In our preaching workshop, Mitch was brainstorming a sermon on Mark 9:38–41. In this text, the disciples are concerned about people who are casting out demons in Jesus' name. Of immediate concern was the theological status of the word *demon* for life today.

> **Elizabeth:** I'm really interested in this verse 39. From my experience in the church, that's what would strike me as interesting. Someone is casting out demons in Jesus' name, and Jesus is saying, "Don't stop them." I mean, the first thing that I think of, from my family history, are some of my experiences with the Southern Baptist Convention. And then I would think about our own denomination now (Presbyterian Church U.S.A.).

> **Burton:** You find that there are demons within these denominations?

> **Elizabeth:** There are lots of them.

> **Burton:** What are those demons? **Use Mitch's theological profile, especially his Relational Mode.** What does it mean to be a demon in this mode? And why is it good to cast them

> Notice that Burton wants Mitch and the entire group to make use of Mitch's theological profile—especially his Relational Mode—to help him think about how an idea in the biblical text relates to our lives today.

out? Where are the demons in our lives? How do we cast them out?

Mitch: For them, in the world of the biblical text and within my theology, I think that **a demon was something internal.**

Burton: What did a demon do when it got inside?

Dwight: It destroyed them.

Burton: We're making progress. Demons are destructive. They do destructive things. All right, Mitch, do you see any destructive powers anywhere? Do you notice any? **Stay with the text, stay with your life, stay with your theology**.

Lee: Well certainly in Mark's world it had something to do with disease.

Elizabeth: And mental illness.

Burton: Okay, demons take people out of themselves. You can use that. You can tell your congregation what demons did in Mark's world, and then use that as a springboard to ask what demons do in our world. Then, you are beginning to get a sermon.

John: Bring your theology to bear as you do this . . . to help you decide what demons are and what they are doing in this world.

> Look at Mitch's reply. It is consistent with his theological profile. For someone in the Relational Mode, demons would not be external, supernatural, or superpersonal beings, but would operate within human hearts to destroy one's relation to self and others.

> The group now uses Mitch's theological profile as a springboard to consider both the biblical text and life in more depth. Notice that theological reflection has to move in *both* directions: toward the text and toward life.

At this moment in sermon brainstorming, Burton has encouraged the class to use the theological profile to help them bring the biblical text and life today into a focused interaction. This conversation proceeded for some time. Because Elizabeth was operating more out of a Social Gospel Ethical-Political Mode, she tended to locate demonic power within structures and institutions, such as religious denominations. After some discussion, however, the class wound its way back around to trying to stand within Mitch's theological shoes, since this sermon is one that he will preach. As already noted, according to Mitch's theological profile, he sees the demonic from within the Relational Mode. The conversation continued:

John: Let's say that the first thing you want to say in your sermon is that there are destructive, demonic forces at work in our world today. All you have at this point is an idea, what I call *semantics*. **There is not necessarily anything theological about it**. Now, how would you frame this idea theologically? How does someone with your **theological profile** think about the demonic? What does the demonic look like within that vision? It's time for a **theological moment.**

> The profile is designed to help you give an idea theological shape, texture, and dimension. Notice the distinction between having an *idea* to preach and having a *theological idea* to preach.

Dwight: Well, anything demonic would be whatever destroys the image of God within us, whatever works against the relationship that we have with God, as well as the relationship that we have with ourselves and with others. **That could include low self-esteem, dishonesty with others, and broken communication.**

> One of the basic theological moments in the sermon preparation process occurs when you begin to shape a *nearly* theological idea into a *clearly* theological idea.

Elizabeth: People divided against each other.

Mitch: Not seeing the image of God in the other person.

> Dwight is now beginning to use his theological profile to unpack the meaning of the demonic in a way that can be preached and clearly understood.

Burton: So the demonic keeps us from seeing that **we belong to each other and to God.**

John: Now we're beginning to get our theology down to the level that anyone can understand. We are finding ways to make the Relational Mode of theology understandable as a way to interpret biblical categories.

> The theological profile's language about *belonging*, from the section on the Relational Mode, is helping to clarify and expand Dwight's thinking about the relationship between the biblical text and contemporary experience.

It is important to note that theological conversation between the text and life does not stop once the issue of the demonic has been identified within both the text and our lives. In order to brainstorm a sermon that will have a consistent and coherent theological grounding, it is crucial that Mitch proceed one step further and *interpret* the demonic theologically for those who will hear the sermon. It is precisely at this point that the theological profile can begin to provide helpful categories for preaching: "broken relationship," "belonging," and so on.

See the Difficult Theological Issues in a Text

Use the profile to help you see the difficult theological issues in a text that need to be preached. Over the years, we have noticed a marked tendency among preachers to avoid or gloss lightly over difficult theological issues, even when those issues are clearly presented by the biblical text. Sometimes, the reason is that preachers want to avoid an intellectual scuffle with parishioners. They believe there are fundamental disagreements within the congregation on a particular subject, and they would prefer to keep these differences under wraps. At other times, tough theological issues are avoided because the preacher has not taken the time to work a theological issue through from start to finish. Preachers fear that this might take too much time out of their busy weekly schedules, or they simply prefer to profess a cautious naïveté about divisive subject matters.

Laypersons have a deep desire to hear difficult and divisive theological ideas interpreted from the pulpit. The average church-goer does not have available the kind or amount of resources on these subjects to which their pastors have access. They look to the pulpit, if not for definitive answers, then at least for a range of possibilities, as well as insights that might help them make progress in their own understanding.

If the lectionary is used, there is ample opportunity to preach nearly every difficult theological issue—divorce, demonic possession, the relationship between Christianity and Judaism, the relationship between Christianity and other religions, the relationship between Christ and culture, betrayal, fear, suicide, death and dying, lust, greed, and so on. If one is not a lectionary preacher, one need only open the Bible to any page, or look around oneself at the culture in which we live to find such issues.

As our class helped Mitch brainstorm his sermon on Mark 9:38–48, it was clear that the class was avoiding an "elephant in the room." One purpose of the theological profile is to help locate these elephants. In verses 39–40, Jesus tells the disciples not to stop a person who is casting out demons in his name, "for no one who does a deed of power in my name will be able soon afterward to speak evil of me. Whoever is not against us is for us." Although the class was willing to say that the power to confront demonic forces in the world is "available to many," they did not seem to want to get into the issue of who *exactly* might be included in this "many." This began to move the group toward a discussion of the relationship between the church and the world, the relationship between Christianity and other religions, and the relationship between the kingdom of God and history.

John: The text seems to be concerned not only with the power to cast out destructive forces, but also with the difficult question of who has that power. **This moves us to other parts of the profile: the Relation of Christianity to Other Religions, the Church and the World, Endings—especially the Kingdom and the End of History.**

> The profile can draw attention to a difficult theological issue in the biblical text that is being missed or avoided, and point to the categories for reflection that are most relevant.

Burton: (Playing devil's advocate.) The text is suggesting that this power to cast out demons is not simply limited to those who say Christ is Lord. That's nice to know.

Dwight: But it says, "In Jesus' name." Would a non-Christian—someone not confessing Christ—do something in the name of Christ?

Burton: No, they wouldn't. But the power is available.

Dwight: The event could happen without them confessing Christ?

Burton: That's what I think the text is saying.

Mitch: No, because he says he is driving them out *in your name.*

Sue: I don't think they have to confess Christ, but when they do that act, it confesses Christ. It's not in the naming of Christ, it is the act itself which is a witness.

Mitch: Verse 38 says, "We saw someone casting out demons in your name, and we tried to stop him, because he was not following us."

Burton: He wasn't part of the church.

Mitch: The structure.

John: **The question remains: Which aspect of your theological profile would you need to consult in order to help you**

preach this difficult concern about who can cast out demons in the name of Christ? If it is not your view of Christ and other religions, perhaps your view of how God's kingdom is at work in history?

> Although the profile can be used to determine which aspect of our operative theology is most helpful for interpreting difficult issues, this is not always an exact science, because it could be several parts of one's profile interacting at once.

Mitch: I'm Dialectical in that category. But I guess I want to go the route of claiming the separateness, of claiming, if you will, certain things for ourselves as the church that nobody else has, whether it be as a church or . . .

Burton: But doesn't the text and your dialectical view of history push against that? Don't they ask you not to do that? Verse 41, *"Whoever* gives you a cup of water."* This text could, perhaps, be worked both ways. The question is, "Is it only the followers of Christ who have the right to this power against the demonic?" This text leaves an opening to say that others have it. That God's power comes through others. The text does not say "anyone," but it does indicate that God's power is available beyond this small community. You see, **for someone with your view of the work of God's kingdom in history, this text pushes you to ask, or at least raise, this question. Are the powers of God to overcome destructive forces available only to those who call upon the name of Christ within the narrow confines of the church?** It's a good question . . . and one that

> In this case, Burton encourages Mitch to examine more closely his Dialectical view of the Kingdom and the End of History. (See Endings.) His theological profile allows for the presence of the kingdom within history, apart from the work of the church. This will help him preach this difficult issue.

people are concerned about. Raise it! And then point out that, for many of us, it is only the community of faith that has this power. That would be another profile: perhaps an other-worldly, apocalyptic, or even realized view. But then you have these words about "whoever is not against us is for us." And that maybe puts a question mark on it—and provides an opening for you to introduce a more dialectical perspective. At the same time, we will be able to see how people in the church can be in real, honest disagreement on this issue.

The issue of who's in and who's out in local congregations and denominations is on everyone's mind and should not be avoided. Mitch's Dialectical view of the Kingdom and the Meaning of History can help him to preach this topic. Throughout this conversation, Mitch was challenged to find the appropriate theological category to preach, to think through his own position within that category, and to discover the way that his theology and the text interact—in this case, with some tension.

Identify Theological Ambiguity and Conflict

Use the profiles to help you identify and understand theological ambiguity and conflict. As we have already begun to see with Mitch's sermon about who has the power to cast out demons, the biblical text, in part because of its largely narrative style, is not always as clear and consistent as a systematic theologian would prefer. There are many theological ambiguities and inconsistencies within the biblical material. These ambiguities should be seen as opportunities to invite a congregation into serious theological conversation. Preachers do not have to be answer people. Often, it is better to raise and clearly define a theological problem, permitting the ambiguities within the biblical text to pave the way for a congregation's own spiritual discernment about the matter.

Sometimes this theological ambiguity exists between the biblical text and our lives, rather than simply within the biblical text itself. In these situations, something within the biblical text, written as it was for first-century congregations, is unclear or untenable in relation to contemporary experience. In our class, Dwight was brainstorming Mark 10:2–12, in which Mark puts these words into the mouth of Jesus, "Whoever divorces his wife and marries another commits adultery against her; and if she divorces her husband and marries another, she commits adultery." Our preachers were disgruntled, to say the least, to think that God would deny remarriage to divorcees, allowing remarriage to be labeled as adulterous. Aren't the consequences of divorce bad enough? And then to have further guilt heaped upon oneself through remarriage! This provided an opening for a lively conversation about the way that authorities other than Scripture influence preaching, especially experience. It also presented an opportunity to see what happens when our own theological profile is in fundamental confrontation with the theology of a biblical text.

Elizabeth: I simply have to **draw upon my experience as an authority** at this point. I know many people who have experienced both divorce and remarriage as redemptive, especially in abusive relationships. Experience looms large in this situation. We know that there can be redemption even though it's not in here (in the biblical text).

> The profiles encourage an awareness of your authorities for preaching. Knowing how the various authorities are at work in your preaching can help you to recognize when they are driving your interpretation.

Sue: But the text is clear. It is calling remarriage adultery. This is serious stuff. **Your congregation may hear this differently—especially those who deny that experience can be an authority at all.**

> Notice how the profiles can make us aware of differences among our hearers that might affect what is heard.

Burton: It *is* serious stuff and maybe you want to say it is adultery. Is that what you want to say?

Dwight: I don't believe it is adultery, and this is *my* sermon we are brainstorming. I affirm my experience as an authority in the same way Elizabeth does.

Burton: (Playing devil's advocate.) **How do you know you're not rationalizing?**

Dwight: I don't know that I'm not. But I know that God's creative Spirit is still at work, so adultery is not the last word here.

> The profiles can be used to help us hear how our theology might be construed by those who adopt another stance. Here Burton adopts the stance of absolute denial of experience as an authority in order to make sure that Dwight owns his position.

Burton: All right. Your theological profile is now in the conversation. Let's see where it takes us.

Dwight: Yes. **Remember that I have a Relational Theism.** I believe that, regardless how broken we become, God is still at work and is still leading us. After the brokenness of divorce, remarriage can be one of the many ways that God's Spirit is guiding us.

> The profiles make us aware of connections across categories within our theology. Notice how Dwight is becoming aware that his view of the authority of experience is not at odds with his understanding of how God is at work in the world. For a Relational Theist, God never withdraws from the world, but is always there, presenting to us possible courses of action that can lead to new and redemptive ways of living.

John: At this point, your experience and your theology challenge the text and are challenged by the text. Now, what are you going to do in the pulpit with this?

Burton: A suggestion. Sermons do not have to solve all problems. You can just lift this up and ask the congregation, "Are we rationalizing when we say this?" And **give them both arguments. Give them the first-century argument and then the argument from your theology**, that you believe that remarriage, in many instances, is living out the new possibilities God is placing before us. Lay it out there, so that people can hear the "yeses" and "nos" within each argument, and leave it as a serious question for the community. Are we rationalizing, or do we really want to affirm Christ's presence in a second marriage? Leave it there and let them decide. Let them see the same stuff you are wrestling with instead of telling them you've worked it through and . . . "Here's the truth." Give the arguments and let them wrestle with it . . . but be sure that you *give them the arguments.*

> The profile has helped Dwight see that, by granting experience a Relative Affirmation as an authority, he will come from time to time into some conflict with the biblical text and, in all likelihood, with some of his hearers. Notice, however, that Burton does not encourage him to override other perspectives with his own or to usurp the authority of the Bible. Rather, Burton encourages him to point out the conflict itself.

Rather than providing a unilateral answer that gives absolute and final authority either to the first-century church's solution to divorce and remarriage or our own contemporary experience and theology, it is possible to set forth the arguments within both contexts, highlighting the problems and ambiguities on all sides. The profile can help you locate and understand these problems and ambiguities. Then, in the sermon, the preacher can open the floor, so to speak, for the theological conversation to continue.

Identify Issues of Theological Authority

The profile will help you identify and understand issues of theological authority. Every preacher assumes various authorities for the messages they preach. Broadly speaking, these authorities are Scripture, tradition, experience, and reason. In part 1, you reviewed the variety of shapes that each of these authorities can take in preaching.

From time to time, preachers need to go beyond simply *using* these authorities to the point where they actually preach *about* these authorities, and *how they have authority*. Many theological problems and issues arise in congregations today because people are not clear about what these authorities are and how they are to be used in the church. Conflicts occur because of the variety of ways in which these authorities are used. Not only do preachers need to come clean about their use of these authorities, but they also need to demonstrate some of the uses and potential misuses of these authorities. Over time, this will deepen a congregation's ability to understand why it is that people of different theological viewpoints think so differently.

One of the members of our class, Steve, is the pastor of a large, urban church in which many of the members are either gay or lesbian. Steve was very aware of how a certain devotional and literalistic way of using the Bible as an authority has been very important to many of his homosexual church members. At the same time, he is aware that this way of approaching the Bible has been used naïvely to exclude and shame gays and lesbians. In his sermon, he wanted to discuss this issue so that his church members could understand this paradox in their midst.

In Steve's theological profile, the authority of the Bible is the Way of Universal Principles, and the authority of tradition is Limited Relativity. For Steve, both the text and theological tradition are shaped by the historical faith of religious communities. He is concerned when texts or traditions are interpreted narrowly—that is, without any awareness of their historical settings.

John: If I hear you right, you are wanting to help your congregation think through the way the Bible and tradition have authority. For you, the Bible and tradition have authority, but not in a boundary-building way—they should not be used to forge identity over and against those who can be scapegoated as "other." **You are concerned about one of the problems sometimes associated with the Way of Verbal Inspiration in biblical authority, and the way of Limited Absoluteness in understanding the authority of tradition.**

> As we have seen, the profile can locate the reasons for a theological conflict or misunderstanding. In this case, the conflict is over the nature of biblical authority and the authority of tradition.

Steve: Yes. I want them to see that traditions and biblical interpretations are more often than not influenced by time and place—in this case, the tradition of violence against what is deemed as "other." **This was not the central tradition within Scripture or the church that Jesus was all about.** Jesus was not about asserting power, judging, or destroying; he was about love. And in the name of that love, he was about nonviolently speaking truth to power, both religious and political. I want my hearers to find the courage to reject the tradition of violence, violence that has been used against many of them, and to embrace the tradition of love, truth-telling, and nonviolent resistance.

> Notice that tradition, for Steve, is granted Limited Relativity as an authority. Traditions are conditioned by time and place and must be reassessed as new truths are brought to light. An attempt is made to find the universal or higher tradition—in this case, the tradition of love, and to make it normative.

By exposing a particular form of oppression within one way of viewing Scripture and tradition, Steve will be able to de-authorize a destructive aspect of biblical interpretation and tradition within his preaching. Since he understands clearly his own profile and the way the Bible and tradition have authority for him, he will be able to do this intentionally and clearly, without entirely undermining the authority of tradition and Scripture themselves. From this, his congregation will learn a great deal about *what* within the Bible and tradition has ultimate authority, and *how* it is that Scripture and tradition have authority for today.

Focus Theological Suspicion

The profile will help you carefully focus theological suspicion. In 1980, Justo L. González and Catherine G. González published *Liberation Preaching: The Pulpit and the Oppressed*. Quoting Juan Luis Segundo, these authors articulate the cornerstone of their liberationist homiletic model in the *hermeneutic circle*:

Firstly, there is our way of experiencing reality, which leads us to ideological suspicion. Secondly, there is the application of our ideological suspicion to the whole ideological superstructure in general and to theology in particular. Thirdly, there comes a new way of experiencing theological reality that leads us to exegetical suspicion, that is, to the suspicion that the prevailing interpretation of the Bible has not taken important pieces of data into account. Fourthly, we have our new hermeneutic, that is, our new way of interpreting the fountainhead of our faith (i.e., Scripture) with the new elements at our disposal.[1]

In order to expose and transform oppressive theological interpretations of Scripture, González and González invite preachers to exercise an ideological suspicion of theologies, biblical commentaries, traditions, and lectionaries in order that interpretations from within the margins of the tradition might come to light. As we have already seen, when preachers suspect that a tradition of interpretation has been violent or abusive, they may decide to de-authorize aspects of that tradition of interpretation.

In one respect, this is a very tricky process. It is tricky because, when placing something that has been abusive or that has caused suffering under suspicion, preachers must be careful not to undermine the authorities for their preaching in the process. Preachers must be very clear regarding what, exactly, is being placed under suspicion, and why. Often this problem occurs when one aspect of a preacher's profile is overriding the one most appropriate to the topic at hand.

In our workshop, this problem occurred several times, especially in the preaching of Sue and Steve, both of whom bring strong Ethical-Political (Liberationist) profiles into the pulpit. For Sue, a concern with the way that some Christian traditions have used Pauline language to support anti-Semitism made her want to indict Paul himself for using language in his letters that opens the floodgates to anti-Semitism. She holds a Forked Parallelism view of the relationship between Christianity and Judaism. This made her very wary of those who carry Supersessionism to the point of anti-Judaism. Burton, however, wondered just how far she should go in placing Paul under suspicion of anti-Judaism. In the last analysis, it appears that another aspect of her profile, i.e., her Ethical-Political Mode, is overriding the category that is most appropriate to her subject matter, i.e., her understanding of the relationship between Christianity and Judaism.

Her text was Galatians 3:23–29. She was especially worried about verses 23–25, "Now before faith came, we were imprisoned and guarded under the law until faith would be revealed. Therefore the law was our disciplinarian until Christ came, so that we might be justified by faith. But now that faith has come, we are no longer subject to a disciplinarian, for in Christ Jesus you are all children of God through faith."

> **Sue:** There's part of me that thinks the same person, Saul/Paul who was able to persecute Christians, that same personality-type, is there, and in a way, I'm wondering, is he now able to go in the opposite direction a little bit and, and he's sort of taking out his frustrations on Israel?
>
> **Dwight:** So you're wondering, "Is he still an abuser—this time of his old faith?"

Sue: Right. I found this concern in several commentaries also.

Burton: But Paul is writing in a different context than ours, isn't he? I mean, in his situation, you've got tiny little Christianity, and Judaism was the oppressor.

Sue: **My Forked Parallelism won't tolerate the hierarchy Paul seems to establish between Christianity and Judaism.** The way that he expresses what he wants to say set it up for us to be in the situation of anti-Semitism that we are in now. His language permits us to merely turn the tables.

> The profile makes Sue aware of where her suspicions are coming from. Sue is only happy with a parallel relationship between Christianity and Judaism, and will be suspicious of language in the biblical text that implies a hierarchical relationship.

Burton: But let's try to get at his understanding of Christianity. For Paul, we cannot do the law. He never says that the law is not God's law. He never says that. The law is God's law. God gave Israel the law.

Sue: (Playing devil's advocate.) It's just dead.

Burton: It's dead in the sense that we don't get salvation through it. There are Jews who would disagree with that. They would say that the law can be done. That's not Christianity. Christianity says that the law cannot be done. **So you do have a difference in faiths. A sharp distinction. Christianity does not have to say that it agrees with everything in Judaism, in order to respect Judaism.** But what we shouldn't say, and what we sometimes do say, is that . . . we are the same. But what he is saying is that we remain God's children even though we violate the law.

> The profile must be carefully exegeted if it is to be useful. Here, Burton points out that a *parallel* relationship does not dissolve *differences*.

Sue: His vocabulary can be misleading.

Burton: But you're completely changing the sociological context. **In your profile, you identify your view of Scripture as The Way of Universal Principles.**

> The profile is often used to encourage consistency in thinking.

This approach to the Bible takes into careful consideration the realities of the historical time and place of their composition. Was Paul supposed to have foreseen the time when the Romans would expel the Jews from Palestine, when Christianity would be triumphant in North Africa and all over Europe?

Sue: But he knew there was tension already.

Burton: The tension was that Christians were being persecuted. That's what he knew.

Elizabeth: (To Burton.) Surely you're exaggerating. You're just trying to put the *best* possible light that you can shed onto Paul.

Burton: Perhaps, but I worry that Paul gets run down in the same way that Augustine gets run down, because we take him out of context and put him into our context.

Sue: I only plan on setting it up this way, by acknowledging that I have a love-hate relationship with Paul.

Burton: But I'm still not sure why. Are you upset by him because he lived in the middle of the first century and spoke in a first-century sort of way?

Sue: Because I think it was irresponsible language.

Leslie: Because his writings have been *used* to support anti-Semitism.

Burton: Then who's irresponsible? The users, or Paul?

Sue: The user. But it still makes me uncomfortable the way he phrases things.

Elizabeth: **Maybe another part of Sue's theological profile is making her drive a harder bargain than she needs to. The way I see it is that Sue has a deep sense of justice that is oper-** ating in the **Ethical-Political Mode of her theological profile. I think that is what makes her so suspicious of Paul.** This makes her worry about the effects of Paul's writing, even upon the Galatian people.

> Often, several aspects of a person's profile are at work at once, creating an interpretation. In this case, Elizabeth draws attention to the way that another aspect of Sue's profile is, in part, driving her way of thinking.

Burton: But isn't the problem what later Christianity did with Paul's writings?

> **Sue:** I'm not so sure. I think that what he did here set the stage for that. As someone operating in the Ethical-Political Mode, I worry about the way in which structures are already in place—in Paul's language and in the church—that will lead to oppression of Jews later on.
>
> **Lee:** What's wrong with being mad at Paul?
>
> **Burton:** Nothing, but in this case, I think he's getting a bad rap.

This argument went on for some time. Sue brings a strong ethical suspicion to both Paul's personality and to his rhetoric. Burton worries that these larger concerns about Paul's personality and language should not be allowed to become overbearing in her treatment of Paul's writings. He wants her suspicion to fall more strongly on the abuses of later traditions rather than on the apostle Paul himself. This will permit her to do a better job of honoring her Forked Parallelism, in which Christianity and Judaism are different branches sprouting from a single tree. The question in this instance is not whether a hermeneutic of suspicion is warranted. The question is what, exactly, should be under suspicion: the personality and expressive language of Paul, or the way that later traditions have used Pauline language. Preachers must be extremely careful when they make these decisions. Otherwise, over an extended period of time, they might undermine more of their own authority than they bargain for. It will also create inconsistencies with other aspects of their theology.

Help When the Text Seems without Good News

The profile can help when the text seems to contain no good news (or bad news). We have already stated that it is sometimes best to take an open-ended approach to theological ambiguities or conflicts. In other words, you do not always have to provide resolutions or good news answers. However, in many situations your theology, in interaction with the whole of the biblical vision, can provide clues to the resolution of these problems. This is especially true when there seems to be absolutely no good news within a biblical pericope. Although preachers must be very careful not to import something that suddenly sets everything right, it is possible for the preacher's theological profile to help the preacher discover clues or trajectories within a text that can be preached as good news.

In our preaching class, Lee was struggling with the "narrow door" text in Luke 13:22–30. At the heart of this passage, Jesus tells a very negative parable in which the owner of a house closes the door to his home, even against those who deem themselves to be his friends and companions. At the end of this parable, the owner says, "I do not know where you come from; go away from me, all you evildoers! There will be weeping and gnashing of teeth when you see Abraham and Isaac and Jacob and all the prophets in the kingdom of God, and you yourselves thrown out" (vv. 27–28). Although Lee professes to be in the Liberationist Ethical-Political Mode, in the theistic worldview section of his theological profile he holds a Relational Theist view of God's relationship to the world. This became the focus of discussion as he struggled to find good news in this text.

Steve: I'm wondering how this "locking out," this permanent "weeping and gnashing of teeth," is affected by your theology.

Leslie: Yes, the door is locked.

Lee: I do think it encourages a certain kind of works righteousness. The hypocrites are shut out.

Steve: **From the perspective of your Relational Theism, there is something that I like in this text. That is, that what we do *matters*. And what we do is not lost on God.** As I understand it, that is an important aspect of Relational Theism.

> The profile can help us locate a positive good news aspect within a biblical text, where one is hard to find. With Steve's help, Lee is able to see that a basic premise of his theistic worldview—that God is intimately connected with the world—can help him find good news in this text.

Lee: Well, that's true. That's helpful. What we do hurts God . . . pleases God . . . affects God.

Leslie: But there's that closed door. It's that closed door that is so scary.

John: If what we do matters to God, what matters most to God? Put your theology together with Luke's theology.

Lee: The welcoming the stranger theme in Luke's theology relates well to my Relational Theism and to my ethical concern for justice. In Luke's theology and in mine, this is one thing that matters most to God.

In this conversation, Lee is beginning to discover how his theology and the biblical vision can help to keep him mindful of the good news, even when the biblical text, and to some extent his own context, conspire to focus him primarily on the bad news at hand. By involving his theology, he is able to begin to discover a theological message in which the bad news and good news work together. One of the most constructive uses of the theological profile is precisely this assistance in seeking out and recognizing the good news that can be preached.

Sometimes, a shift to a new theological category within the profile can open up the positive (or negative) dimensions of a text. Elizabeth, struggling with the Joseph story in Genesis 45:3–11, began to recognize that the story is not only conveying bad news but also good news, then more bad news, then some good news, and so on. When she shifted from one theological category to another, the deeper rhythms of sin and grace in the story came into view.

Elizabeth: **What I see all over this text is social sin**. This fits the Ethical-Political Mode in my theological profile. But I also want to see God at work in this situation, helping to bring about some redemption for each of these characters. I don't see it

> The profile has many parts. If we are overly negative or positive by using one category, we may overcome this inclination by shifting categories of reflection. Notice how this happens.

happening just for Joseph, and I don't see it happening in a way that is perfect.

Burton: For that reason, I think if I were you I would just go back and forth. In this moment in the larger story, verses 3 through 11, you have a nice moment in the midst of a not-so-nice story. There is betrayal, alienation, hatred, violence, abuse of power, and so on. Go ahead and name them. Because, remember, you are also going to name them in our own lives. Let your theology help you name them.

Elizabeth: I can do that.

Burton: **But remember that you indicated to us that you have a Dialectical view of history.** All of us do have nice moments. To be realistic, therefore, you have to preach that redemption as well. . . . But notice, the Bible is much more realistic than we sometimes are. There's terrible stuff

> In order to overcome an overly negative reading of the biblical text, Burton wants Elizabeth to move from her Ethical-Political Mode into another category of reflection: Endings, in which she can reflect more deeply on her more optimistic understanding of the kingdom of God in history.

coming, including Joseph and all of his ancestors being enslaved . . . real abuse. **From within your ethical perspec-**

tive, there is much more in the way of social sin yet to come in this story. Egyptians enslaving another people. Serious exploitation of a marginal group. Lay that out for us to hear also. If you do that, we

> Notice that Burton switches back to her Ethical-Political Mode to highlight the negative aspects of the text.

will get the clear message that the God at work in our lives is the God who is trying to draw us out of all that. The way the Bible tells our theological story has a stark realism to it that we should not lose when we get to talking about our own lives. The same kinds of social structures are wielding abusive power in our lives. The way the Bible tells the story, and **as your Dialectical view of history emphasizes,** God is

> Then, by shifting back to the category of Endings, her profile can help her see the positive aspects of the text as well.

always at work in the real world seeking to move us out of all that, or to overcome all of that. And there are real moments when we move out, when that stuff is overcome. But then, you know, we are going to move back.

What Burton wants Elizabeth to see is that she does not have to end her sermon with either all bad news or all good news. The theological rhythms of biblical faith and of her own theology are far more complex than that, and sermons should bear this out wherever necessary.

It is especially easy for preachers who preach from lectionary texts or smaller pericopes to allow their interaction with only a few biblical verses to limit their theological vision. It is even possible for preachers to become almost obsessed with one or two verses within a larger pericope, and to lose sight of the larger biblical witness within a pericope itself.

It is also possible to narrow one's theological vision based on one's immediate life experiences or the very particular issues confronting a congregation. It is typical for preachers to preach whatever it is that they are down under at a particular time.

In light of these concerns, it is important for preachers to learn how to recognize when they have become too narrowly focused in sermon brainstorming and to look for clues that will lead to ways to break free from this tunnel vision. These clues can only be discovered by pushing back from the immediate text, and from one's immediate life-issues, and assessing the big picture.

One word of caution should be observed, however, when doing this. When confronted with problems or double-binds within the text of the Hebrew Bible, Christian preachers quite often push back from the text too far and import a "Christ is the answer" solution into their sermons. Although there may be significant theological clues in the person and work of Christ to answer problems or issues within the testimony of the Hebrew Bible, it is very likely that these same clues could be found within the Hebrew Bible. Rather than moving historically to Christ, preachers can use their Christian theology to help them see new aspects of hope within the Hebrew Bible itself. This will help Christian preachers avoid a tacit or explicit anti-Judaism in their preaching.

At one point, while discussing Elizabeth's theology of the Joseph narrative in Genesis 45:3–11, the class was down under the problem of tribalism and ethnocentrism that seemed to be motivating Joseph. Based on her exegesis, Elizabeth decided that Joseph was acting from enlightened self-interest: to protect his family and tribe. This sparked a heated conversation about various negative forms of tribalism and scapegoating in our world today. This included not only ethno-religious tribalism, but all of the pervasive and insidious in-group/out-group dynamics at work within schools, churches, denominations, public institutions, corporations, and so on. In considering what Elizabeth could preach, the group was having a difficult time finding its way out of this problem.

Burton: **Since you have the Social Gospel Ethical-Political Mode in your profile, Elizabeth, it would be natural for you to look way ahead of the story of Joseph to Jesus saying "everyone is my brother and sister," which breaks the power of the tribe.** Now, you wouldn't want to do that at the level of actual history, because it is Supersessionist, and that's not where you are. But you do have to recognize this impulse within your theological vision. As a Social Gospel preacher, you cannot help but think about the kingdom of God, where tribal loyalty is not enough. This kingdom is inclusive of all.

> The profile can help Elizabeth rise above her negative concern with tribalism in the text. Burton points out that her Social Gospel Mode will help her see a larger vision in which to re-frame the Joseph story.

Steve: Okay, with that theological vision in the back of our minds, if we come back to the story, we can see how this tribalism of

Joseph's fails. As the story continues, there's that other episode of Joseph basically enslaving everybody and being able to enrich himself and his family by using the famine.

Sue: Yes, the narrow tribalism, motivated by fear, doesn't seem to go very far in this story. And by the end, the only one who is really blessed by this is Jacob. But, in a way there's a symbolic restoration of the promise, and it is conferred on Jacob and his ancestors. **The story, then, ultimately reminds us of a larger, more important reality beyond the tribe—the** *promise* **and the** *covenant.*

> Sue helps Elizabeth find two themes that she can relate to her Social Gospel perspective.

Elizabeth: Perhaps my Social Gospel perspective, then, can help me discriminate between potentially violent forms of tribalism in our lives and living as bearers of God's expanding *promise* **and** *covenant.* That, it seems to me, would be a helpful distinction to make in today's world . . . and one that stays within the scope of the message of the Hebrew Bible.

> Now Elizabeth has begun to use her Social Gospel perspective to discover a larger frame of reference.

In this conversation, we can see a mixture of Christian Social Gospel theology, the faith narrative of the Hebrew people, and real life issues in today's world. Elizabeth's theological profile becomes a way of helping her go back into the larger biblical narrative within the Hebrew Bible in search of theological clues that will help her resolve the issue that she is down under. She does not have to feel compelled to run all the way forward in the biblical narrative to the person and work of Jesus Christ. Her Christian theology, however, which we presume is rooted in many ways in Jewish theology, can help her know how and where to look within the text, to themes of promise and covenant, and to similar places within our lives, for insight.

Decide What Kind of Information the Biblical Text Provides

Use the profile to help you decide what kind of information the biblical text is giving you. It is a common mistake for theologians to treat a metaphoric text as if it were history, an apocalyptic text as if it were predictive, an existential text as if it were metaphysical, the mythical text as if it were factual, and so on. One of the first questions a theologian must ask in the process of sermon brainstorming is: "In light of my theological profile, what kind of information is this text giving me?" This question became crucial at one point during the brainstorming of Lee's sermon, as the group reflected further on the words "There will be weeping and gnashing of teeth."

Burton: With a text like this and with other texts also, for instance, the rich man and Lazarus, you have to ask yourself, "What kind of information am I getting here? Am I getting metaphysical information?" That is, when I look at the rich man and Lazarus, is that a text about the nature of reality? Is that telling me that there's a hell and a heaven? You see, if you think that what we have here is a metaphysical text, that Jesus is telling us a little story to give us hard information about a second dimension of reality, that is, that there's another life at the end of this life, and in that other life there are those that suffer and "gnash their teeth," and there are others who are in a state of bliss. **If that is so, then perhaps you have an Other-Worldly understanding of the kingdom of God from the Endings section of the profile.** That's what I mean by a metaphysical text. Is that what we have here? Or, is Jesus telling us, "Strive!" Is he giving us a word about how we can live? **In that case, this text matches your profile, where you profess a Dialectical view of the kingdom of God and history.**

> The profile can help you decide what kind of text you are dealing with. Here, Burton points Lee toward the aspect of the profile that will help him make this decision: his understanding of Endings, or the kingdom of God in relation to history. Although stories such as the Rich Man and Lazarus have been used to support an Other-Worldly view of the kingdom of God, Burton encourages Lee to notice the word "strive" in this text (v. 24). This word invites him to make use of his dialectical view of history to interpret the story.

Steve: With some hyperbole in it. (Laughter.)

Burton: I would say so. This text can match your Dialectical view of history and the kingdom. It is a text that is telling us how we should live now in order to participate in the coming kingdom. The parable is a way of bringing out the point that it really matters how we live now rather than giving us metaphysical information.

The decision about what kind of theological information the text is rendering makes a tremendous difference for preaching. This decision will have a great deal to do with how you decide which part of the profile is most relevant to interpret the text at hand. This is the kind of question that should be asked early on in the course of your theological work with a biblical text.

Think Through an Idea, Issue, or Problem

Use your theological profile to help you think an idea, issue, or problem all the way through. It is not enough to simply identify a theological idea and leave it at that. For instance, to say to oneself, "here I'm dealing with sin" will not be helpful, unless the meaning of sin is thought through carefully in relation to the subject at hand. It is here that it is crucial to return to part 1 of this book, and to other resources, in order to think the theological idea through to a point where it is helpful for the sermon you are working on.

As Dwight worked to put together his sermon on divorce and adultery from Mark 10:2–12, he was aware that, in his rural southern church, there would be much individualism and perfectionism. The North American religious context is one in which ideas of individual perfectionism and purity have strongly influenced the way sin is typically preached. The idea that we are embedded within a larger fabric of sinfulness in which we can always expect a certain amount of brokenness, alienation, and active sinning tends to get lost in much of North American preaching, especially within traditions that have been influenced by revivalism. Knowing this, Burton encouraged Dwight to make use of his theological profile to think through the meaning of *original sin* within his theological profile in relation to the idea of divorce in his sermon.

Burton: Do you see that, in this case, acknowledging the sinfulness, the fallenness of all things is actually helpful? **Your Relational Mode can help you here.**

> Burton draws attention to Dwight's Relational Mode, which acknowledges the universality of sin.

Steve: But you remember Jimmy Carter got in trouble with that sort of thinking. It's not all that popular in the American context.

Elizabeth: So you don't want to say that Jesus is condemning this sin of divorce?

Burton: Jesus always condemns sin. He is saying it is sinful.

Elizabeth: So where's the redemptive word?

Steve: He's an equal opportunity condemner of sin. (Laughter.)

Burton: That's not far from right. We've already noted that this text does not come on strong with words of redemption.

Sue: **But there is something at least slightly redemptive in the awareness of the larger context of brokenness within which the particular sin of adultery takes place.**

> Notice that the group begins to see that, once the idea of original sin has been thought through completely, there seems to be some help for preaching.

Burton: Right, the point is that a doctrine of sin tells you that our situation is broken. Pure, absolute love, sheer obedience to God is not a real thing, it's just not real. And that's the problem with those sermons that say, "Do this!" "Do that!" They're not being real.

Steve: **That's, in a sense, liberating**. The fact that sin is embedded within the fabric of reality itself is a kind of releasing thing.

Burton: Absolutely.

Steve: I like it when William Sloan Coffin says—and I think he overstates it—that the doctrine of original sin was the most optimistic doctrine in the world.

Burton: I completely agree.

Steve: Because you don't have to live up to this unachievable perfection.

Burton: And you don't have to go around telling yourself all the time that you're bad. You are bad, but it doesn't have the same effect. This is who we are. This is why we need God. This is why we need forgiveness. This is why we need repentance. This is why we need love from others, not for what we do, but just because we are brothers and sisters in the same situation. Don't judge me by my works. This is why we are free, Luther says, because you are not going to insist that I be lovable, in order to love me. God doesn't insist that I be good, in order to love me. You see, this is the Christian gospel. That's the beginning of the good news in this text, that someone can say: **"Even though I'm divorced, God's going to love me, and give me a chance to get going again . . . get into new relations."**

Leslie: So you can't say that if you hadn't been divorced, you wouldn't be broken.

Burton: Right. But if you have other sermons in which you tell people that they can live unbroken, then divorce is a terrible sin. Because you're saying that I really could live unbroken.

> The profile provides Burton with an opening to help Dwight think theologically about sin in relation to this text on divorce. He has to *think sin all the way through*, in order to get to the place where he can begin to see its implications for this sermon, in the Relational Mode.

Leslie: We're broken every time.

Burton: That's right. That's why it's called original sin, as opposed to notions that there are "sins." When you think of sin as if there were a list of sins, then you can tick them off and say, "I won't do this and I won't do this." But if you think of sin in relation to sinfulness, in your theology—**relational brokenness**—then what we call "sins" are a manifestation of this deeper original sin, and these manifestations are endless. That doesn't mean that we can't knock off some of them. We do, that's one of the things that we can do with our lives.

Steve: That's one of the great things about Niebuhr's work, I think.

Burton: Absolutely. **Original sin works across all of the theological modes, from Transcendent to Relational.** That is, if they are to be preached in a way that is true to the apostle Paul, and to the theology that came out of the Reformation.

> The profile has highlighted what happens when we bring a specific perspective to a doctrine that is shared across the theological modes—and then follow that theology all the way through.

In this conversation, Burton helps Dwight to work a figure-ground reversal on the way that particular, individual sins are typically considered in his congregation and in his preaching. This can only happen, however, if he is willing to use the Relational Mode from his profile to help him think the problem of divorce all the way through in relation to the larger category of original sin.

Think Through Different Pastoral Issues

Use the profile to help you think through the same theological category in relation to different pastoral issues. Perhaps the most important theological question to ask when brainstorming a sermon is, "What pastoral issue is it, precisely, that I am dealing with?" One way to sort this out is to let the theological profile be your guide. Ask yourself which category from the profile should guide your reflection. Then ask yourself what pastoral issue you are dealing with, as precisely as possible, so that your hearers will not become confused.

While brainstorming Dwight's sermon, it was important at one point to distinguish clearly between two pastoral issues: divorce and remarriage. The text presented Dwight with a set of problems, because the text deals with both of these as sinful. Although both pastoral issues might be dealt with within the context of a theology of sin, and especially original sin, each of these pastoral concerns requires its own very particular theological consideration. Divorce is the ending of something. Second marriage, after a divorce, is the beginning of something. Although both are laden with the consequences of human brokenness, each one opens toward grace in a very different way. Within Dwight's relational understanding of sin and atonement, second marriage could be seen as opening toward a very particular set of new relational possibilities.

Burton: **The profile has given us a theological context in which to think about divorce: sin. But remarriage is a separate pastoral problem.** This is not just talking about divorce. This is talking about remarriage. In your sermon, make sure that you don't confuse them. There are two different issues here. We've established that Christianity is not a ruthless moralistic religion. Christianity knows our brokenness, and identifies that brokenness, and this is Jesus telling us that we are broken, defying God in this way, just as we do in a thousand other ways. And the good news is that God loves us, forgives us, and moves us to reconciliation. We've established that. You could stop there.

> Notice that the profile articulates the larger theological context, but each pastoral issue brings with it its own peculiar problems and emphases.

John: Yes, that is certainly one option. It is better to be clear, and to deal with only half of a text, than to leave your hearers in confusion.

Sue: But I think you have to deal with it.

Burton: You have to be careful, then, because, if you will have already preached a redemptive word about divorce, then you don't want this to sound like a little appendix.

Dwight: **Keeping my Relational view of sin and atonement in mind, I think that remarriage has within itself both the difficult consequences of sin, and a real possibility for new forms of belonging, and loving relationships.** Remarriage seems to hold within it more in the way of grace than divorce, because divorce leaves one's future dangling. This would have been true in the first century, as it is true today also.

> Dwight and Sue use his profile to begin to think about the relationship between sin and grace in remarriage.

Sue: The broken relationships—sinfulness, original sin—within divorce carry over in many ways into remarriage. Step-families are not easy. To be true to the text, we have to make sure that this brokenness comes through in our sermon. What you have is starting over, a fresh start, new life, and sinfulness, with all of its consequence, all wrapped up together.

Dwight: I guess that my Relational view of the atonement always places brokenness, and the potential for grace, next to each other. Making choices is important within my theological worldview. But the knowledge that I am caught up in sin does not overwhelm or shut out the possibilities for grace. God is still at work, still leading us, still giving us new opportunities for redemption.

In this conversation, Dwight is learning to use his theology to reflect more deeply upon both the similarities and differences between distinct pastoral issues as well as the ways that each issue informs the other. Each issue presses his theology and the biblical text in different ways. Thankfully, at this point Dwight is (1) working with the correct theological categories for his subject matter, i.e., his Relational Mode and view of the atonement; and (2) keeping the pastoral issues raised by the text and by his theology distinct from one another.

Homiletic Theology Builds Up the Church

By now, you should have become aware of how the theological profile can be used to bring about a variety of theological moments during sermon brainstorming. There are many other uses for the profile, but we will leave those for you to discover on your own. One final word is in order, however, before we move on to the business of sermon writing.

Preaching is a part of the overall ministry of the church. All proclamation, therefore, is in service of building up the church universal. It is entirely possible to brainstorm sermons that tear church people down with shame, ridicule, and criticism, and by undermining authorities. Whenever preaching loses its theological and ecclesiological vision, it becomes a platform for ideologies and moralism, and the edification of the church can be left far behind.

At the heart of every sermon brainstorming session, the preacher should constantly ask, "How can this message build up the body of Christ?" "Where is the redemptive power in this message for the people of God?" One of the most consistent threads of conversation in every workshop where we have used this method is a discussion of the relationship between an emerging sermon and the goal of strengthening the wisdom and vision of the church. One might even say that this concern undergirds every part of the sermon brainstorming process.

It is with the church and its welfare in mind that we turn to the business of crafting sermons themselves. This is appropriate, because it is at this point that preachers turn from coming up with something to say to finding a way to say it that will lead their congregations with theological imagination and vision.

Chapter 4

The Theological Profile
and Sermon Composition

The second set of theological moments in your sermon preparation should occur during the composition of the sermon itself. In this chapter, we have included excerpts of conversation that relate directly to the business of organizing and writing sermons. These excerpts illustrate some of the ways you can use your profile once you actually begin to write a sermon. Again, we have included commentary to highlight some of the ways the profile can be helpful.

Get the Theology into the Language of the Sermon

The profile can help you get the theology you want to preach into the language of the sermon. It is not enough to *think* theologically, as important as that is. The theology that you think must find its way into the language of your sermons. This does not mean that you use "theological language," the kind of abstract language found in theological textbooks. In some instances, with explanation, textbook language can be used. For the most part, however, you will need to find a way to break theology down into categories and ways of speaking that can be understood by your hearers.

It is crucial to remember that using biblical or theological words without *explaining* them is to avoid the theological task in preaching altogether. Preachers are forever telling congregations such things as "live Christ-centered lives" without explaining who Christ is, or "the Church is a Spirit-filled community" without defining in any way what is meant by the word *Spirit,* and so on. Simply using the big words of the Bible or the tradition in a sermon is not to be theological in preaching. Theology must provide a clear and concise *interpretation* of these categories. For a sermon to be theological, it must take the categories of faith and interpret them, using language that is understandable and meaningful in a particular congregation. The profile can help you begin to find this language.

In our workshop, Mitch was wrestling with how he could improve the first sequence of his sermon about the demonic. He had not yet moved beyond simply using the word *demon* or *demonic* in his sermon, to the place where an *interpretation* of the demonic was being offered.

Mitch: Where am I missing the theological language?

John: That is an important question. You have to be sure that you encode theology in your sermon. It doesn't just happen. You might start your sermon saying something like, "There are demonic forces in the world." Even though you've used a big, theological-sounding word, *demonic,* you have actually said nothing theological yet. **It's time for another theological moment. You have to push back and ask yourself, "Using my profile, how am I going to help these people understand the meaning of the word *demonic*"?** And so you go a step further, as someone in the Relational Mode, and you say something like, "The demonic enters into human life whenever we live as if we do not belong to ourselves, to one another, and to God. Whenever the fabric of relationships is broken, the demonic enters." Once you have said this kind of thing, you have begun to interpret the demonic and to preach theologically. These are not complicated words, or words that people cannot get at. But if you don't have those words in there, in the sermon, then you have no theology at all.

> The profile can help you begin to find the right language to speak. Here, John uses Mitch's profile to begin the process of teasing out words he can use in his sermon to speak about the demonic. This is one of the most important theological moments in sermon preparation.

Mitch: So it is a matter of defining terms. Interpreting them.

John: Exactly. Or you might think about it as rounding out the theological ideas in your sermon.

Mitch: So at each point along the way in my sermon, I have to push back and ask, "What would the Relational Mode that I operate with say about this"?

Burton: Yes. You have to ask, "How can my theology help me and my congregation to understand and locate the demonic? How can it help us understand what and where demons are?"

In order for preaching to be theological, the theological interpretation of biblical and theological categories must become a part of the *language* of your sermon. You cannot assume that people know what these categories and ideas mean. You have to tell them.

Do Theological Reflection *Before* You Illustrate

If possible, use the profile to help you do theological reflection *before* you illustrate your sermon. We have noticed over the years that preachers tend to begin searching for illustrations before they have done theological reflection. We would argue that there is no way to know how to illustrate a point until you have decided on the full theological meaning of the point you are making. This is true whether you plan to preach inductively or deductively. In Mitch's sermon, for instance, he will only begin to think of precise illustrations or experiential reference points for his interpretation of the demonic once he has decided, theologically, what the demonic actually is.

John: **A theological moment is absolutely crucial before you start naming things in our lives that correspond to your idea.** You don't know what to go to until you have done the theological work. Once you have named the characteristics of the demonic from within your Relational theology, then all kinds of things will start to come to mind regarding what the demonic looks like in our experience. Then you will start to name things in human life that represent the demonic.

> Notice that another theological moment in sermon preparation should occur before and during the process of illustration.

Sue: I think that this is the step that we forget. We tend to run to human experience before we do the theology.

John: Right. You have to stop at each point along the way, ask the theological question, answer it, and then you will be able to *see* what you are talking about in human life. Human experiences will just start to spill out. **Once you say that the**

> Using the profile will help you see what kind of sermon illustration you need to use.

> **demonic is that which "breaks the fabric of relationships,"
> all kinds of things begin to come to mind within our culture,
> within our own lives, within our congregations.** Someone
> with a Transcendent theology or an Existentialist theology
> would define the demonic differently, and that will mean their
> sermon illustrations would tend to be different as well.

In order to illustrate sermons in ways that are congruent with your theology, you must pause for theological reflection whenever you begin the process of sermon illustration. There is simply no way to know how to illustrate sermons in a way that is theologically consistent and coherent without this kind of integrated theological work.

Use Dialectical Thought and Language

If your profile calls for dialectical thought and language, be sure to use them. There are very few areas of life or of theology in which there are no gray areas. Oddly enough, however, when many preachers enter the pulpit to preach, most of the subtleties, inconsistencies, and synthetic qualities of life tend to be left behind. In fact, the pejorative meaning of "preaching at" someone in our culture today is precisely a form of rhetoric in which either/or reasoning is at work. Although there are categories within the profile that call for the jettisoning of dialectical thinking (Church against World, for instance), most of the categories require some form of dialectical thinking in order to be consistent.

In order to think dialectically, pay careful attention to the things you are affirming or rejecting. Whenever you are saying "yes" to something, you should also ask, "Where is the 'no' in this?" Whenever you are saying an emphatic "no" to something, you should stop and ask, "Where is the 'yes' in this?"

One of the best test cases of dialectical thought and language within the theological profiles is in the Church and World category marked Church as Transformer of the World. Many preachers indicate a preference for this category, whereas the rhetoric of their preaching indicates something to the contrary. In our class, this occurred in a sermon by Leslie, who had indicated that she subscribed to Church as Transformer of the World in her profile. While discussing her sermon, however, the class felt that her sermon language and illustrations supported a Church against the World position.

> **Mitch:** With the Church and World portion of your profile, I'm not sure
> about your approach. It seems to me like Church against the

World, but you say that you are a Church as Transformer of the World theologian. You preach against the "culture's system of oppression and power" as if the church could somehow escape that system.

Leslie: **I meant to use Church as Transformer of the World. But I may not have done that well. Where does my language go wrong?**

> The profile can help you to see where you need clarification and consistency in the language of a sermon. Leslie professes a Church as Transformer of the World theology, but the language of her sermon sounds more like Church against the World.

John: You tend to use language about culture that is world-attacking— a kind of separatist or Church against the World language. Maybe it comes from your context. You use the word *culture* where a revivalist preacher might preach against *the world*. In the language of your sermon, people are either in the church or in the world, but never both at once.

Burton: You see, the transformationist has to be dialectical and use dialectical language. There are a number of aspects to being dialectical, but at least one of them is that, for whatever you find in culture, there is both a

> Notice how important it is to be aware of dialectical thinking and language as you craft the *language* of a sermon.

"yes" and a "no." And that's opposed to the Church against the World model, where culture, by definition, is always to be negated. The transformationist finds something wrong *and something right*. The transformationist seeks to qualify the wrong, though we know, when we are through qualifying, there is still going to be another "yes."

John: If you're conscious of this, you'll watch these sweeping phrases, "Christ says," "the world says," "in the world," "worldly," and so on.

Burton: The transformationist knows that we are a living lie. We are up there with our fancy clothes on, we've just left a house that costs more than a hundred thousand dollars, driving our nice automobiles; we're way up there on the socioeconomic ladder in this country, and then simply to get up there and to preach these unqualified anti-culture sermons . . . we know it is problematic.

    Sue: Isn't that what we're supposed to do? What are we supposed
          to do?

  Burton: Be dialectical, if that's your theological ethic. Have a little
          sense of moral and theological ambiguity in the pulpit. Dialectic
          is hard. If you're going to be dialectical, you're going to have to
          be conscious of it. You've got to always ask yourself, "I've just
          said 'no,' where's the 'yes'?"

The overall effect of dialectical reasoning is the avoidance of oversimplification, and the forthright and realistic portrayal of moral, theological, political, and social ambiguity. This is not meant to soften the "no" that should exist in preaching. Neither is it meant to sap the energy out of our "yeses," our affirmations. Rather, it is designed to show that these negations and affirmations are neither easily held, nor unrealistic and naïve.

Organize the Theological Ideas

The profile can help you organize and order the theological ideas in your sermon. As we have indicated, theology is filled with complexities and subtleties. Sometimes, when working with theological ideas, preachers can get hung up on these complexities, believing that they have to deal with all of them immediately. This can create serious problems for sermon writing. In order to deal with these complexities, a preacher may try to wrap them up in a single movement of thought in a sermon. This, as it turns out, is simply an impossibility. What tends to happen is that a kind of semantic drift occurs in which sermon listeners lose track of the core theological idea and begin to drift down one or more of the complex tributaries the preacher is trying to explain. It is very important that preachers learn to stick with an idea until it is finished.

Remember that the complexities within an idea should have been thought through during sermon brainstorming, so that these minutiae do not have to show up during sermon writing. By the time the preacher is writing the sermon, the way the idea itself is expressed should already contain or express the complexity the preacher desires the congregation to hear. If it is necessary to further unpack the theological idea, this must become a new movement of thought entirely in the sermon.

This brings us to what is perhaps the very heart of this issue: *theological patience.* Preachers tend to know what the further developments of an idea are, so it is difficult to rein in the desire to cover everything at once. In some instances, this promotes a kind of circular logic whereby preachers race ahead and divulge something of the good news to come, or circle back to explain something they forgot to deal with. It is important to remember that this kind of circular logic has a way of "erasing tapes." Racing forward or backward in a theological argument tends to erase everything in between. Remember that listeners to sermons can only be in one theological place at a time. You can use the profile to help you determine where you are theologically and when you should move on.

As our group of preachers helped Mitch brainstorm his sermon, they came up with a three-part division for his sermon: (1) There are destructive, demonic powers in the world; (2) there is a power in Christ to cast out these forces; and (3) this power is available to many within and beyond the church. As should be obvious by now, the class spent a good bit of time brainstorming the idea of the demonic, theologically and experientially.

Leslie: We spent a lot of time on this problem of the demonic. I'm wondering about this "casting out demons in your name" part of the text (v. 38). I'm wondering about this business of who has the power to cast out demons. I'm worried about the immediate assumption by some that we are only talking about Christians.

John: But that is the third movement of thought in the sermon that we are planning. We still have to finish this idea, then complete our second section on the power of Christ to cast out demons, and only *then* will we get to the issue that you are concerned with. **We've used the Modes and the Theodicy sections of the profile to think through the *problem* of the demonic. In the third part of the sermon, we will move to the Relation of Christianity to Other Religions section of the profile. Try not to jump ahead when you write your sermon,** and you won't tend to lead people in circles when you preach. People can only be at one place at a time, and it will help you in your sermon writing if you only allow yourself to be at one place at a time, theologically, as you write.

> The profile can help you to define the boundaries of each movement of thought in a sermon. The profile will also help you to give each movement of thought adequate theological space in the sermon before moving on.

Of course, there is an issue of how much of each of these ideas you want to put in your sermon. That is another issue. You

> may not want to spend as much time unpacking the demonic, or
> working through how it is that Christ casts out the demonic.
> This is an issue of balance or the relative weight that you give
> to each idea in your sermon. But what I am trying to say is that
> you can only be in one place at a time. Be patient with your
> ideas. Finish one before you move to another.

No matter what your theological profile, this issue of theological pacing
and patience is important for the crafting of sermons. It will help if you will
discipline yourself to (1) work through theological complexity before you
state your theological idea and (2) patiently work with one theological idea at
a time in your sermon.

Preach the Good News as Good News

The profile will help you preach the good news as good news. For a variety
of reasons, some preachers fail to communicate any motivating good news in
their sermons. From our experience, there are several reasons. Some preachers seem to cave in to the culture's pejorative definition of *preach,* and thus
feel the need to sound "preachy." Sermons are loaded with hard or soft imperatives: "we must," "we should," or "let us," and "we are called to . . ." These
preachers are reminiscent of the hospital nurse's "we need to take our medicine now." Other preachers worry that the congregation is not doing all it
could to support the preacher's exciting vision for church growth or social justice. These preachers feel compelled to nag at their congregations for their
failings. Still another set of preachers has lost sight of the redemptive good
news altogether. They are lost in doubt, based on a lack of theological confi-
dence or conviction, and thus can only muster a few hints and helps for daily
living as a positive message on Sunday morning. Another group of preachers
is angry about something within the congregation or culture at large. They feel
the need to load up on people week after week, dividing the sheep from the
goats.

There is certainly plenty of bad news in the world, and the good news that
we preach should not appear Pollyannaish. With this in mind, we still feel
compelled from time to time to remind preachers that the heart and soul of
preaching is the good news of God's redemptive grace and mercy. Whether
one is preaching a text from the Hebrew Bible or from the New Testament,
we are fundamentally in the service of a God of redemption and hope.

During one of our conversations on this topic, Burton made use of the profiles to offer this advice:

Burton: **Love, like any other redemptive reality, has to be placed within a theological frame-work.** Otherwise, we are likely to preach it as a moral com-mand—as more bad news. Your profile can help you find this theological framework. For a Liberationist, or for that matter, a Social Gospelist, love is elicited by an experience of

> Using the profile can help you discover how love, justice, forgiveness, and so on can be conceived *theologically* instead of moralistically.

God's vulnerability in relation to others. Within a Transcendent theology, and to some extent, the same is true within an Existential or Relational theology, love is elicited as the result of forgiveness. Without this frame, the good news you want to preach may turn sour.

Telling a person to love is yet another impossible command. Forgiving them for not loving actually opens them to love. I assume that is the Christian message. Because we are loved, and we experience the vulnerability of others, we love. We don't love because God tells us to love. Whitehead is good on this; he calls this "God the ruthless moralist." Love! Love! Do justice! Do justice! Do this . . . do that! This is God coming on as the moralist. Not much good news here. Don't command people to love; open up the love of God to them.

We assume that one of the fundamental gifts theology brings to preaching is that it can help preachers to escape preaching moralism and find the good news. This was *the* fundamental issue Luther had with preaching in his generation, and it remains one of the fundamental issues for preachers today. The goal of a sermon is not to sound "preachy," but to sound a resounding note of grace.

With this in mind, we invite you to write only a theological vision that inspires you and will inspire your congregation. It is easy to finish several hours of exegesis only to arrive at a completely flat, moralistic, and insignificant message. Ask yourself whether your message is theological good news for your own life and for your congregation before you proceed to write your sermon. At the same time, examine your motives. Be sure that neither anger nor your church administrative agenda is motivating your preaching. Instead, you should make certain you are motivated by the desire to preach a word of grace and hope.

Although there are occasions and biblical texts that call for an imperative word from the pulpit, it is best to avoid both the hard and soft imperative voice in preaching unless it is first grounded in the solid indicative of God's grace. Weed out the language of "must," "should," "ought to," "let us," and "we are called to." Instead, try to use the language of identity, possibility, process, and vision. Give the strong impression in every sermon that the church is a powerful agent of grace living more deeply into its redemptive identity and purpose every day. As Burton pointed out, in most cases, you cannot simply command people to love or forgive or do justice. Help them discover these things as a part of their *identity* as redeemed persons. Be sure to let your profile help you to find the theological framework in which redemptive realities can be voiced *as redemptive*, rather than as further condemnation (for not loving, forgiving, or doing justice well enough).

Correct Overly Individualistic or Social Tendencies

The profile can help you correct overly individualistic or social tendencies in your sermons. We assume there are individual, social, and, indeed, cosmic dimensions to all of the theological modes within the profile. Typically, for the Existential and Transcendent preacher, the focus is on the individual. Those in the Ethical-Political and Relational modes will more typically focus on society and social relationships.

In every mode, we encourage an expanding, broadening form of illustration. Telescopic illustration moves from the micro to the macro and back again. In order to illustrate a sermon telescopically, the preacher must first of all ask, "What are the individual dimensions of this theological idea?" "What are the social dimensions?" "Are there cosmic dimensions?" With each of these questions, the preacher can use the profile to recognize tendencies toward the individual or the social and think the idea at hand toward a mixture of these arenas of human life.

Leslie: **I would think that the existentialist's style of preaching would naturally accentuate the individual.** Wouldn't it be more likely, in an existential sermon, to hear illustrations and stories in which individuals struggle with sin and grace?

> The profile can help you to identify the way that illustrations are sometimes skewed and become primarily individualistic or social.

John: Generally speaking, I think that is true. But existentialist theologians would also want us to keep the social dimensions of anxiety, loss of meaning, and grasping after less than ultimate concerns in mind. **Existential sin at a social level looks a lot like idolatry, doesn't it?** Grasping for things to secure us in the world: consumerism, materialism, etc. And the best way to communicate the interwoven qualities of the micro and the macro is in our illustrations.

> Although some profiles are more individual or social in nature, each profile will have both of these dimensions. Be sure you identify both of these dimensions in your profile.

Burton: You will have people out there who think of sin only in terms of the personal. There are personal ills and personal solutions. And there are others out there who think of sin only in structural terms. In Mitch's sermon, for instance, there are those who will think that the demonic powers can only be broken through personal faith. And others will be thinking more about the social and structural dimensions of evil. But if you give illustrations throughout that come from all over, **illustrations that are consistent with your existentialist way of thinking about evil, but that still engage structural evil, then you are talking to every one of those people in your congregation,** and you are getting them talking to each other. You are both affirming them and encouraging them to listen for other dimensions of their faith.

> Burton points out that illustrations can be a good place to reach across profiles and communicate with those who occupy other theological positions.

We encourage telescopic thinking when it comes to both your ideas and your illustrations. In this way, both the individual and the social dimensions of your theology will be preached every Sunday morning.

See Your Way Before You Write

The profile can help you see your way through theologically, before you start writing. The best purpose of a good sermon outline is to help the preacher determine whether he or she will be able to see a trajectory of thought through from start to finish. It is a sad and all too common experience for a preacher to realize in the wee hours of Sunday morning that neither the text being preached nor the theology being used to interpret the text will suffice to answer the theological question being posed in this Sunday's sermon. If this had been determined at an earlier stage, by using an outline or by working things through as carefully as possible, it would have saved a lot of trouble once the sermon was in the writing stage. Once you have begun to write your sermon, you may find that you have committed yourself to a direction of thought that you cannot complete. At this stage it is often too late to repair your compass and to move in another direction.

At one point in conversation with our preachers, Burton was responding to questions about a sermon he had preached for the class. Members of the class worried that the theological question Burton had put to the text did not seem to be an obvious one. This could easily have left him dangling, with no "Word" from the text to help him answer his question.

> The profile can help you keep track of the things in a sermon that are unresolved, point to resources that can help resolve them, and indicate when they are unresolvable.

Burton: If I did go to the text and, having wrestled with the question I was putting to the text using my theological profile, I didn't find an answer, then I would obviously have to do something else. Before I start writing, I'm thinking about this. I don't start writing until I'm sure I have somewhere to go. I'll think for three or four days before writing. I don't start writing until I have the whole structure of the sermon in my head. I'll walk the dog for hours, read various things, think about it. I would not say that you can automatically expect to bring a tough question to a text and have it answered. I'd like to say that. But I don't think I want to say that. If I found that I couldn't address this question, if my hunch about this text was wrong, if my profile was not helping me or was in hopeless conflict with the text at the level I was pursuing, then I would have to do something else. When I see a way through, that "seeing" for me is where I know I've got a sermon.

One of the most helpful things Burton says in this excerpt is that he knows he has a sermon once he has been able to work an idea through in relation to the text, his theology, and his life experience in his congregation. It is likely that one of these three elements will have to be short-circuited if he begins writing too soon and then discovers he is unable to see his message through to the end. This, of course, is unacceptable.

Write Strategically When Preaching for Theological Change

The profile can help you write strategically when preaching for theological change. Although we would argue that it is always important for you to preach a consistent and coherent theology, it is not always the case that you should feel compelled to persuade others to adopt this theology. Certainly, over a period of time, this may occur anyway. There are times, however, when you will feel compelled for pastoral and practical theological reasons to attempt, over time, to bring about a significant change in the theology of your hearers. Here are several strategies to use when writing sermons that are designed to persuade your hearers to change their theological positions.

1. Allow for authentic faith among those who are in fundamental disagreement with you.

As the theological categories should make clear, a significant range of perspectives has been held on most important theological issues in the church. When another person is in fundamental disagreement with you, you can acknowledge this disagreement without questioning the integrity of their Christian faith. One of the most fundamental principles of communication is that you must care for your hearer if you desire to communicate a difficult or threatening idea. This is very difficult to accomplish, especially when you feel very strongly about a particular theological issue. Awareness of other legitimate theological profiles can help you to acknowledge disagreements without questioning another person's theological integrity.

Lee: Our congregation is simply surrounded by churches that hold to an inerrantist view of Scripture. While there are some areas that I can agree on with these people, I simply have to tell them that I think they are wrong on the issue of the ordination of women.

Elizabeth: That goes for me, also. They are just wrong, and it has to be said. What else can you say about that?

Burton: And you have some of these people in your own congregation?

> The profiles will help you to become aware of differences between your theology and the theology of others. In this case, there is a significant difference in the understanding of how Scripture has authority. This difference has led Lee to a pastoral decision to preach for theological change.

Lee and
Elizabeth: Yes.

Burton: Then, as far as I'm concerned, inasmuch as you say that in a way that questions the integrity of their faith, I think you are in the wrong, as well.

Elizabeth: But their faith is wrong.

Burton: No, they have faith in Jesus Christ, and in this situation, you strongly feel that they've made a mistake. Do you make mistakes?

Lee: Of course.

Elizabeth: Sure.

Burton: Then, **to say that somebody has gotten something wrong should not necessarily extend to the integrity of their Christian faith.** Of course we all disagree with people on things. Does that mean that they are not really Christians? If someone is doing something wrong, you accomplish very little by telling them off. What you really want to do is to move them.

> Burton encourages Elizabeth to see that it is possible to hold a legitimate perspective within the range of options provided by the profiles, and to still make mistakes. Recognizing this should not lead us to question the integrity of someone's faith.

Elizabeth: But I don't want to *validate* them.

Burton: Validate them as Christians with integrity of faith. That's all I'm asking for. You don't have to validate this particular belief to validate the reality of their faith.

Elizabeth: I have a hard time seeing the difference between validating their faith and validating these beliefs.

Burton: Let's try an analogy from another realm of experience. Let's say we are having an election. You may be a Democrat, and you absolutely hate the policies of the Republican candidate. Are you going to question the morality, the responsibility, the "Americanness" of those who choose to vote for the Republican candidate? Do you question their desire to do what is best, to make a responsible decision about the future of this country? No, as misguided as you believe they are, you cannot question the basic Americanness of their decision.

Lee: Is this just blind pluralism?

Burton: No, I'm just saying that people, no matter what their theological profile might be, make mistakes, and I am among them. It is quite another thing to say that "because you hold this position, I question your faith."

The kind of baseline acceptance that Burton is asking for does not come easily. This is especially true when the theological issues that divide us are issues that threaten our identity or livelihood. Nevertheless, the acceptance of the basic integrity of another person's faith is absolutely necessary if you desire to change another person's mind. It will be far easier for another person to accept that they have made a wrongheaded decision, acting in good faith, than to accept that their identity as a Christian itself has been a sham all along.

2. Rehearse your own struggle and process of change.

In many instances, you will have gone through a significant process of change yourself in relation to certain theological issues. In order to negotiate a hearing for the position that you now hold, it will help if you work inductively. Invite your hearers to join you in a process of discernment, growth, and change instead of drawing lines in the sand. Most basic theological changes take time and involve a reconfiguring of one's authorities as well as one's life experience. Your own personal testimonial can be helpful as a way for others to see how this theological reconfiguration takes place.

Burton: There are times when your congregation needs to know not just where you are coming from, but *where you have been,* theologically speaking. **It will help them to hear something of the way in which you came to hold positions in your profile that you now hold.**

> The profiles can be used to help articulate where you have been theologically, and how you got to where you are now.

Steve: So using the theological profiles is not just a matter of laying out where we are and then saying, "You respond to that."

Burton: That's right. At times there will be so much dissonance between where you are and they are, that they will need to hear how you got to where you are.

Because of the ways our theologies and our identities are caught up together, difficult theological change must be linked to changes in identity. For this reason, the struggles, difficulties, threats, adjustments, and insights that the preacher has experienced along the way can be of tremendous assistance. The best way to do this when preaching is to present your own personal narrative in such a way that you do not wear a hero-hat. Rather, present yourself in the role of an often inept, sometimes stumbling, but always learning and changing disciple. This will give your hearers a chance to come alongside of you in a process of further development and ongoing discernment.

3. Change is a often a matter of semantics.

A major part of theological change involves erasing certain meanings within theological discourse and then reclaiming that semantic space and filling it with new meanings. For instance, one large semantic category within Christian discourse is the category of sin. Let's say, for example, that you are working to move your congregation from the Transcendent Mode within the profiles to the Existential Mode. Part of what you are doing, over time, is phasing out a transcendent theological semantics of sin and phasing in an existentialist theological semantics of sin. You will cease to use the language of pride and willful disobedience. Instead, you will substitute the language of finitude, anxiety, and the grasping after idols. If this change is matched by changes in other areas of church life—Sunday school curriculum, hymn books, mission statements, liturgy, and so on—then it is possible, over time, to bring about a significant change in the way that sin and other theological categories are understood within a local congregation. Within your preaching, this will require a sustained editorial vigilance. You will need to review every sermon in order to be certain you are working consistently to reclaim these vital semantic spaces.

Differentiate Your Theological Message

The profile can help you differentiate your theological message from others, in order to achieve clarity. There are times when you need to tell people what you are *not* saying, in order for them to understand more clearly what you *are* saying. In other words, you need to identify theological ideas that run counter to (alongside or over against) your idea in order to clarify what you are saying. This is an especially important thing to do when the range of different profiles among your congregation leads you to believe that your hearers are interpreting a word or phrase differently, or that they might be desiring you to move in a different direction in interpreting an idea than you plan to go.

At one point during our class, Elizabeth was aware that, when she used the word *Satan* in her sermon, she would have to be very careful in her context in a small, rural church that the meaning of this word was clear. From within her Ethical-Political Mode, the word *Satan* referred to various forms of structural sin and evil: evil as it manifests itself within political, corporate, and social institutions, especially as they are influenced by systems of money and power. In her congregational context, however, the Transcendent Theological Mode was mixed together with a Supernatural Theism and a Christus Victor theology of the atonement. For many of those listening to her sermons, therefore, the word *Satan* referred to a very personal and supernatural form of evil. Satan was a very powerful, spiritual being who worked in a variety of ways against the better wishes and conscience of the individual.

Elizabeth: In my context, where Satan is a personal demon, and people are invited on every street corner to subscribe to something called a "plan of salvation," many of my hearers believe that, when it comes to the demonic, Christian theology can only be Transcendent, Supernaturalistic, and shot through with a Christus Victor or Substitutionary theology of the atonement. I find that I have to be very clear when I use biblical words such as *Satan*.

John: It is likely that you will need to make use of counterpoint in your preaching. **That is, you will have to say over and over again, "This is not what I am saying," or, "What I am saying is this, *not* this."** You will have to do this so that your frame of reference does not slip back over into their frame of reference. You are not necessarily saying, "This is where we all have to be," but you are saying, "I want to be very clear about what I am saying."

> The profile can help you to clearly differentiate the theology you want to communicate from those that you do not want to be heard. This sometimes requires counterpointing the theological profile you suspect many of your hearers will bring to your sermon.

Elizabeth: So I would actually say something like, "When I say the word *Satan,* I am referring to an evil power within society and institutions, not a personal, spiritual demon"?

John: That's right. All that you are saying is that "We are not going there this morning. We are not talking about that, we are talking about this." In that way, you will achieve far more theological clarity in your preaching.

It is likely that Elizabeth will need to make use of counterpoint in her preaching many times. In this way, she will establish better control of the kind of semantic drift that occurs during preaching. Most people, unless instructed otherwise, will simply run the categories that you are using through their own interpretive grid. Counterpoint is a way of arresting this process and inviting people to track more closely with the theology you are actually preaching.

Edit, Edit, Edit!

It makes sense that our final word in this chapter on sermon writing is to advise you to edit your theological ideas before you preach them.

John: The theology that you preach is all in the language. It is in the choice of one word and not another, to leave out one word, and to use, and reuse, another word.

Dwight: But it just seems like that would take all day, every day. It would take so many more hours to think about all of that.

Burton: Not really. Mostly, it is taking things out. **You get rid of things that you don't want. Then, you replace them, consistently, with the things from your profile that you do want to say.** It doesn't make your sermons bigger. It's just that you don't say things in one place that will contradict what you are saying in another. It's not that you say everything in every place, it's just that you don't say some things, and then say something else later on that doesn't make any sense in light of what you just said.

> The profile will help you edit the actual words you speak so that you are clearer and more consistent theologically.

The good editor is always asking, "Does this make sense?" "Is the argument consistent?" "Is this really needed?" "What will help to clarify this point?" It is absolutely crucial to ask these questions with your theological profile in the forefront of your mind. We encourage the theological edit as the last thing you should do before beginning to practice delivering a sermon. This is the only way to insure that the final draft of the sermon really conveys the desired theological message coherently and consistently.

Chapter 5

Two Sermons

Here we provide two of our own sermons accompanied by brief comments. This will help you see exactly what theology looks like in sermons, and how you can use your profile to analyze sermons you have written or preached. It can be an enlightening exercise to analyze several of your sermons to see the ways your theological commitments are at work (or not at work) in your preaching. It will be helpful to have the Theological Profile (Short Form) on hand as you read these sermons, in order to remind you of the categories we reference in our comments.

Sermon One

The first sermon was preached by Burton Cooper on June 30, 2002, at St. Barnabas Episcopal Church, Norwich, Vermont. The congregation is small (perhaps one hundred worshippers on a Sunday morning); for the most part, highly educated and economically well-off; white, liberal, and a mix of "childrened" families and relatively active retired professionals.

The lectionary text was Genesis 22:1–4, the story of Abraham's obedience to God's command to sacrifice Isaac. This is always a problematic text to preach from, and its difficulty was compounded by the times, which were not good. September 11 was with us in a thousand depressing ways, corporate greed scandals were surfacing, the president had begun his campaign for war on Iraq, and the economy was remaining down. The preacher's mood was low. Although he has existential sympathies, his commitments to Process modes of thinking (relational, dynamic, hopeful regarding the future) normally dominate his sermons, especially their conclusions. That is not true in this case, though the preacher had not consciously noted or intended it. The post-sermon typological analysis revealed that the sermon's ending is strictly existentialist. Was this for better or worse? He thinks that it weakened the sermon, that he allowed his low mood to diminish the hopefulness of a gospel faith.

〰〰〰〰〰〰

Genesis 22:1–4

> After these things God tested Abraham.
> He said to him, "Abraham!"
> And he said, "Here I am."
> He said, . . .

And then comes the terrible command that sets the story in motion.

Abraham was once considered a model of faith, and in many quarters still is. But he has become a troubling figure for those of us who, though people of faith, are also people with a modern, Western cultural consciousness. For we value freedom and equality for all people, we oppose the oppression of women, and we see as a great evil the abuse of children. The Abraham who appears in this biblical story, and others, one of which was the casting out of Hagar and Ishmael, which we heard last week, (this Abraham) is set in a culture with a very different consciousness and different social values from ours. Here hierarchy is accepted as the established and natural, even divine, order of things. Abraham's place in the hierarchy is as the family patriarch with unquestioned authority over his wives, children, workers, and slaves. Not our cup of tea.

> The preacher grants authority to our own experience in a Relative Affirmation. He then points out a tension between that authority and the authority of culture and experience within the biblical text. This also sends the message indirectly that the Bible has authority by way of Universal Principles, or as God's Fresh Address. We will not be adopting biblical ideas through direct, literal translation.

We know that this story means well. It's intended to demonstrate the authenticity of Abraham's faith and, perhaps more centrally, to encourage the people of Israel to continue to trust God even when trust appears senseless because everything is going wrong. One could preach on these things, and I've heard and read many good sermons on this story,

> The preacher deepens the tension by attending closely to the problem that the text sets up for us today. The hearers are invited to follow along as this problem is solved.

but no matter how good the sermon, what I remember afterwards is that God asked Abraham, just to test him, to do the worst thing that a father could do, and that Abraham was ready to do the worst thing that a father could do. In other words, I get overwhelmed by the details so that I lose the intent of the story, just as someone can't see the forest because they are in the midst of the trees. I don't think I'm alone with this problem. So this is what I propose to do. The only way to see a forest when you are in the midst of the trees is to keep on walking past the trees until you come to a field. So the way I want to preach this morning is to keep on working on the details until I come upon the gospel.

Let's take the first troubling detail: that God should suggest a human sacrifice as if a human sacrifice is an appropriate act of religious faith. It is not only we the readers who are taken aback by this. Whoever it was 2,600 years or so ago that collected or edited these stories of Abraham and put them into the written order that we have in today's book of Genesis was also troubled by this demand. How do we know this? Because the editor begins the story with an editorial comment, assuring the reader that what they are about to read is only a test, not the real thing. Look at the first line on your lectionary leaflet. "After these things God tested Abraham." It's a statement put in by the editor to make the transition from the previous Abraham story and to ease the horror of the coming one. Now the editor knows very well that no modern Israelite living in 600 or 700 B.C.E. believes that God would require human sacrifice, but he also knows that those Israelites would be aware of the religious practice of human sacrifice in the distant past of the ancient world, and perhaps even in the distant past of some of their remote ancestors. In other words, those Israelites were aware of something that perhaps we have forgotten: that human beings are capable of sacrificing the lives of other human beings; that even parents are capable of sacrificing their children on the altar. The Bible tells it like it is. The Bible is a book of faith, but it is a book of faith that holds a mirror up to us, so that in its stories we see the ways that we relate to each other, we see the things that we do and that we believe, for good

> The preacher maintains the tension, pointing out that it would also have been present in biblical times. The Bible is not God's dictated word (The Way of Verbal Inspiration). It is human words that reflect and describe our faith in God (either The Way of Universal Principles or The Way of God's Fresh Address).

> The preacher doesn't want the hearer to believe something just because he says it is true. Note how the preacher relates reason to faith. Our reasoning and faith mutually modify each other.

and for ill. If we think of the Bible as a mirror, then we have a clue to the other troubling details of this Abraham-Isaac story.

Any feminist analysis of this story finds it wanting, not so much for the way women are depicted in it, but because they are not depicted at all; they don't count enough even to be depicted in it. Sarah may be the wife of Abraham who has heard an amazing command from God, and she may be the mother of Isaac who is the disastrous object of this command, but as far as the story goes, Sarah is left in the dark. She doesn't count in the telling of this tale. And why doesn't she count? Because the Bible is here holding up a mirror to ancient life where by and large women were the subordinate sex who didn't need to be consulted on weighty matters such as the sacrifice of their own children. Some feminist analyses fault the Bible for upholding patriarchal values that discount women. But the Bible is not upholding these values; it's simply telling us

> The preacher appeals to the experience of many in his congregation as an authority through a Relative Affirmation of feminist ideas. He also continues to carve out his view of biblical authority. He grants feminist critique, but also wants to preserve the authority of the Bible by pointing out that the Bible describes faith instead of issuing timeless decrees.

that human beings, even those who are the people of God, are capable of holding these values, of discounting each other. The Bible does not make decisions for us. We are the ones who have to decide, according to our understanding of faith, what is the appropriate way for men and women to relate to each other.

Let's turn to the last of the troubling details: the binding of Isaac. Isaac says, "Father . . . the fire and wood are here, but where is the lamb for a burnt offering?" So Isaac has a clear understanding of what a burnt offering is. He knows what's at stake. His father answers: "God himself will provide the lamb for the burnt offering." The text doesn't tell us whether Abraham believes this or whether he is simply deceiving Isaac in order to avoid a scene. If we think that no person of faith, at least in the biblical tradition, could conceive of God allowing the death of a child in order to test the faith of the father, we need to remember that other story of God testing a person of faith, the book of Job, where God authorizes Satan to take the lives of Job's children. Again, I am talking of the Bible as a

> Here the preacher completes the argument about how the Bible works: as a mirror of our conceptions of God. The congregation begins to hear that a new way of understanding the Bible might lead to a new way to solve our problems with this (and other) Bible stories, in which the ways of God seem unduly interventionist, coercive, or even violent.

mirror of our conceptions. The Bible not only reveals to us who God is and how God acts, but also mirrors for us who we think God is and how we think God acts. It's up to us to discern the difference—not always easy, and we fight about it. There are still people today who think that God authorizes floods, or forest fires, or an AIDS epidemic, or airplanes crashing into tall buildings.

Our story continues. Abraham "bound his son Isaac, and laid him on the altar, on top of the wood. Then Abraham reached out his hand and took the knife to kill his son." Isaac loses his voice here; the knife is raised over his head, and he has nothing to say. Not even a cry. In a way, he becomes like Sarah. We know he's there. We know he cares deeply about what's going on, but all is silent. The storyteller isn't interested in Isaac's thoughts or feelings. The details of Isaac's state of being do not matter, do not count, in the story. But they matter to us, just as the details concerning Sarah matter to us. We need to ask ourselves, why.

The answer is simple. We think Sarah is a person; we think Isaac is a person. They are persons just as Abraham is a person—and we get offended when Abraham or the storyteller does not treat them as persons. Abraham hears God's command, he rises early the next morning, saddles his donkey, takes his son Isaac and two young men, cuts some wood, and rides off. Where is Sarah? We know she's there, just as we know the house is there, and the furniture is there. And that's what bothers us. In the story, Sarah's there in the same way as the house and furniture are there. Abraham says nothing to the house and nothing to Sarah. He is treating her as a thing. Sarah is a living soul, a mother with passions and hopes, with a will of her own, but in the story she's like a thing. Silent. The same is true for Isaac, only more so. Abraham binds Isaac, and then lays him on the altar, on top of the wood. Isaac might as well be a piece of wood himself. Abraham uses force. He binds Isaac, picks him up, lays him down. Not a word out of Isaac, not even an entreaty. Isaac is pictured as a nonresistant element, a thing, just as Sarah is pictured as a thing. The idea of a person being a thing is a logical contradiction. Yet what is impossible in logic becomes true in life. The terrible thing about this story of Abraham and Isaac is not that it happened—there are few biblical scholars who think we are dealing here with an historical event—no, the terrible thing is not that this happened but that it is true. There are times when we treat others as things, ignoring them, even inflicting

> Here, the preacher's theology enters in order to help solve the problem. His Relational Mode reframes the text so that we can begin to see sin as "treating persons as things." This is true in the story, and it is true in our own lives. To exist is to be relational, and yet sin, the denying and breaking of relationships, is a part of our common destiny.

violence on them; and there are times when others treat us as things. How else do we explain the laughter, the sheer glee, of the Al Qaeda leaders as they watched film footage of the fiery collapse of the World Trade Center buildings, and how else do we explain our calmness, our sense of satisfaction, in watching film footage of one of our megabombs exploding in a remote cave in Afghanistan filled with Al Qaeda fighters? The contradiction of persons becoming things is lodged within all of us—and when we reflect upon it, it can tear our souls to shreds. We would like to deny it, or at least not face it. But perhaps all of us by the very fact of being born are destined, at one time or another, to be treated as a thing and to treat others as a thing; to suffer violence, psychological and physical, at the hand of others; and to inflict violence, psychological and physical, upon others.

This morning's story ends with the unbinding of Isaac—the release of the human spirit from violence, from force, from being treated as a thing. And that too is a truth. There are times in the history of the human race when communities have overthrown social structures that violate, degrade, and humiliate human beings. The practice of slavery, once so prevalent in civilized communities, accepted even by Plato and St. Paul, Washington and Jefferson, is now almost universally condemned, practiced only in

> Here the preacher introduces a Dialectical view of history (see: Endings). The kingdom is present in part within history itself. We see real achievements. And yet, there are always new injustices to overcome.

remote, hidden corners of the world. The subordinate status of women, once the norm in all societies, is being rooted out in the West and becoming an issue almost everywhere else. In our country, we more and more direct our social and legislative energies toward minimizing the negative effects of racial, ethnic, and religious prejudice. Even so, the terrible events that we are now living through—the horror of 9/11 and the continuing threat of radical Islamist terrorism, the misery that Israelis and Palestinians are inflicting on each other, the nuclear brinkmanship of Pakistan and India, the fear that there are nations and individuals willing to use biological weapons—(all this) remind(s) us, as if we need reminding, that it is the human lot to be threatened by violence, to be plotted against by someone, somewhere, as if we were things, and, in response, for the sake of safety and security, it is the human lot to threaten others with violence, to treat others as things. Is there any end to this? Is there any good in this? How does our faith help us to see, to live with hope?

The good in this comes from the realization that we share with all others the common lot of finding ourselves treated as things and treating others as things. The traditional Christian way of saying this is that we are all caught in the bonds of sin. The world does not divide up into the good ones and the evil ones, the righteous and the unrighteous. Of course there are degrees of goodness and degrees of evil, but none of us is foreign to doing good, and none is foreign to inflicting evil on others. We are

> Although the preacher is developing an individual ethic of faith, he rejects a Church against the World model.

fellow creatures sharing responsibilities for both the miseries and goodness of our lives. The sense of being fellow creatures is a precondition to seeking love and justice for all people, not simply for a select few.

But our faith does not simply point us to sin, as the basis of our sense of fellow creatures, but points us to Christ as the basis of our hope for healing and reconciliation. In Christ, human suffering is laid bare. Christ, in whom the divine spirit dwells, is nailed to a wooden cross as if he too were a wooden thing. Christ hanging, helpless, immobile, unable to move his arms or legs, hardly able to talk, degraded, humiliated, violated, feeling abandoned, forsaken by God. We sometimes say that Christ suffers as a punishment for our sins, that Christ had to pay the price of our salvation. But perhaps it is not that way at all. Perhaps it is just the opposite. Perhaps God is not giving us Christ as an offering for our sins but giving us God, present in Christ, suffering, for our sake, the suffering that afflicts us all—in order to

> Notice that the preacher moves from a Dialectical theology of history into an Existential view of the atonement. This is not inconsistent, but it does lead to a darker, more measured, and individualistic understanding of redemptive possibilities in a post-Holocaust, post-9/11 world than would be found in the preacher's professed Relational view of the atonement. This decision is a response to the times.

reveal the love of God for us. Just as a child realizes the depth and healing power of a mother's love when he sees his mother suffering because he is experiencing pain, so in the suffering of Christ we see the depth of God's love for us and experience its healing power. The experience of God's love for us in the crucified Christ does not lift us into a utopian world. The world we live in remains a place where force and treating others as things is prevalent and sometimes necessary, even morally responsible. But in Christ, we know that it is not force but God's love that is at the bottom of all, that love is the very reason for our existence, and the purpose for which we live, no

> The sermon could have moved into a hopeful, relational, and ecclesial ethic. This was prepared for by the Dialectical view of history. Instead, the sermon moves toward an Existentialist and individualistic ethic. The profile exposes this shift in focus and highlights the power of current world events to shape homiletic imagination.

matter what else is going on and what else we may have to do. In the Gospels, Christ tells us to seek the kingdom, that is, seek love and justice, above all other goods. And in today's Gospel reading (from Matthew 10:42) Christ says, "whoever gives even a cup of cold water to one of these little ones" shall have their reward. Just so. Just so. Even a cup of cold water can be an act of love, treating a person as a person, releasing their spirit from violence and violation, unbinding them as Isaac was unbound, so that they too can live a life open to God's love, and open to going out to others with an act of love. Let it be so with us. In Christ, let us live in order to give a cup of cold water. In Christ, let us live in order to unbind Isaac. Thanks be to God for God's great mercy. Thanks be to Christ. Amen.

Sermon Two

This sermon was preached by John McClure at Crescent Hill Presbyterian Church in Louisville, Kentucky, on January 27, 2002. This is a mid-sized congregation of around 250 highly educated members, located in an older suburb near the city. The congregation is moderate to liberal theologically and politically. Members are mostly middle income, somewhat racially mixed, and represent all ages and family situations.

The primary biblical text for the sermon was John 14:1–14. The sermon was preached as part of a sermon series on the person and work of Jesus Christ. The series was a response to a larger denominational concern regarding the uniqueness of Jesus Christ. The Presbyterian Church (U.S.A.) was wrestling with this issue at the time, and a position paper would be ratified at the General Assembly on the subject in June of that year. John 14:1–14 was a central biblical text under discussion by the denomination. Although the preacher's Dynamic Pluralism in the category of Relation of Christianity to Other Religions is clearly at work throughout the sermon, it is ultimately his Existential Mode that provides a way through the impasse created by the seeming exclusivism in verse 6: "No one comes to the Father except through me." In a way, this circumvents the issue. It is, however, consistent with the pastoral setting (of despair and hopelessness) within the text itself.

∞∞∞∞∞∞∞

John 14:1–14

Let's begin by asking who is God and who is Jesus, according to this Bible story.

Well, this is a God who has a "house" in which there are "many dwellings." God is a big Habitat-for-Humanity–type God who loves to welcome folk to a place that contains many dwelling places, or what the KJV calls "mansions" under one endless roof . . . sort of an infinite hotel.

> The preacher immediately reassures the congregation that he is ruling out Radical Exclusivism as a way to approach this biblical text.

And Jesus, who is "in the Father," in the habitat-welcoming-God somehow, and who has this habitat-welcoming-God "in him" is, so to speak, a chip off the old block—nothing short of God's welcoming agent in the world. Jesus goes so far as to imply that he is something like a personal real estate agent and house warmer who goes on ahead and is busy preparing a dwelling place for all of the people that he has been welcoming.

We cannot understand the rest of the story, unless we understand these two things:

> The biblical text seems to presume a Transcendent Mode. The preacher honors this at this point, but does not commit to a transcendent theological interpretation for the entire sermon. (The presupposition of this book is that any text is open to a multiplicity of theological interpretations.)

- God is a habitat-welcoming-God, a God "of many dwelling places."
- And Jesus, who has this Father "in him" and is "in" this Father, is the welcomer to at *least* one of these dwelling places . . . the one he is preparing for his followers.

Now let's move on to the scene in which John's Jesus uses this language to describe himself and God. If we go back a few verses, we hear Jesus saying these kinds of things:

> "Very truly, I tell you, one of you will betray me."
> "Little children, I am with you only a little longer."
> "Where I am going, you cannot follow me now; but you will follow afterward."
> "Very truly, I tell you, before the cock crows, you will have denied me three times."

Jesus is unfolding the final script for his life—of betrayal, suffering, denial, and death—but worst of all—of leaving, of farewell, of no more face-to-face relationship, no more touching, no more teaching, no more healing, no more hope. And Jesus can tell that his hard words have left his disciples, hearts troubled. They are worried about the future, desperate for words of hope, words of life.

The scene, then, is of a ragged, tired, and scared bunch of disciples with terribly troubled hearts. That's the scene for Jesus' powerful, soothing, and hopeful speech.

> The preacher, operating in the Existential Mode, is seeking to establish an existentialist context for Jesus' words. This requires struggling with the text, to some extent, because the text accentuates Jesus' divine foreknowledge of coming events.

"Do not let your hearts be troubled. Believe in God, believe also in me. In my Father's house there are many dwelling places. If it were not so, would I have told you that I go to prepare a place for you? And if I go and prepare a place for you, I will come again and will take you to myself, so that where I am, there you may be also. And you know the way to the place where I am going."

Jesus is speaking a deeply personal word of comfort and hope for real future contact with him. He's not just preparing a room, but he's going to be there too: "*I will take you to myself,* so that where I am (in our dwelling place in God's infinite habitat), there you may be also" (emphasis added).

I remember hearing these same words of comfort and welcome several years ago at my father's funeral: And when they come from Jesus to a troubled follower, as they did to me on that terrible afternoon in Birmingham, they felt like someone reaching out and wrapping me in a warm blanket, I can tell you. To hear Jesus say, "Do not let your hearts be troubled. Believe in God, believe also in me." To hear Jesus say, "I will take you to myself." Simple, crucial words of reassurance at a bad time of life. That was enough for me.

> Note how the preacher's Existential Mode breaks through here. The preacher uses a moment of existential despair in his own life in order to elicit similar moments in the memory of his hearers.

But, for some reason, it doesn't seem to be enough for Thomas. You know Thomas. . . . He always has one more question. Something in me wants to elbow him and say, "Ssshhh!"

But Thomas always has to ask another question. He just has to say what's on his mind: "Lord, we do not know where you are going. How can we know the way?" I mean, if Thomas had not asked that one question, we'd never have had to deal with verse 6—the troublemaker verse—the one that has been used to proof-text arguments and justify atrocities from the middle ages to today. Dare I even speak it? Well, here goes.

Jesus said to him, "I am the way, and the truth, and the life." So far so good—this is more of Jesus reassuring them—telling them that they can trust him and continue to follow him.

But then he says IT. *"No one* comes to the Father except through me" (emphasis added). Uh-oh. Does this mean that no one comes to God except by knowing and believing in and naming Jesus as their personal Lord and Savior? That's the exclusivist line—Jesus is the exclusive, only, and unique pathway to God. No room for Buddhists in God's habitat.

> The preacher now moves into another theological category: The Relation of Christianity to Other Religions. The sermon is being preached in a liberal congregation where the exclusivist way in which this text has been used is deeply troubling. Also troubling is the way it has spawned debates. He gives some indication of the range of the debate, showing how divided the church is on this subject.

Then there is the inclusivist line: Does it mean that no one comes to God except by knowing and believing in and living according to the divine Word or Logos, the Christ-pattern who, like wisdom in Proverbs 8, pervades the universe and can be found, to some extent, in all religions? That's the inclusivist line. Some Buddhists are included, because we can see Christ in some of them, some of the time. But, believe me, inclusivists and exclusivists are only the tip of the argumentative iceberg. There are the hierarchicalists, and the radical pluralists, and the dynamic pluralists, and so on and on.

But wait a minute, slow down. Once again, let's come back to our scene. The scene for this story is not one of debate about other religions on the floor of an ecclesiastical assembly. In fact, there is not another religion in sight or mind. Just these frightened disciples. Thomas is not at all concerned about the salvation of Zoroastrians. He and Philip and the rest of the disciples are looking for hope . . . and for comfort. It is Philip who picks up Thomas's refrain: "Lord, show us the Father, and we will be satisfied." There is a note of hopeless desperation in his voice: "Just *show* us the Father!"

> The preacher responds to the problems raised by this biblical text by reasserting his existentialism. The Existential Mode breaks through both the Transcendent Mode within the text and the overlay of Relation of Christianity to Other Religions sometimes placed on this text. The preacher is now providing an existentialist analysis of the disciples' dilemma. Jesus' departure does not lead the disciples to question whether other religions are pathways to God. Rather, Jesus' departure is triggering Thomas's and Philip's negative consciousness: desperate uncertainty.

These are young men, true seekers after God, in desperate need of certainty and comfort, and Jesus stays with them, does not reject them, and offers them his deepest and most reassuring welcome.

I was talking about this text to a friend the other day. He's not exactly an every-Sunday, front-pew Christian. He has his share of doubts. He's well educated and knows that John's Gospel was written late in the first century, and that the language is loaded with John's theology of the risen and ascended Christ. He knows that none of this language would pass the Jesus Seminar's litmus tests as the actual words of the historical Jesus. In his own words, "Verse 6 is the beginning of the modern sound-bite." You know what he said, though, about this story of Jesus and Thomas and Philip? He said: "When I read a text like this, more than trusting what is *said*, I trust what is *happening*." He went on to say: "It's how they treat each other that is most telling." And what did he see? He saw the disciples as honestly seeking for answers to the deepest questions in their lives. And he sees Jesus bending over backward to offer them an answer . . . the biggest answer possible for them . . . real hope, comfort, a sense of place in his presence—with him—no matter where he goes, and no matter what terrible things may happen in the days to come.

> Notice the appeal to reason in this section. The Way of Mutual Transformation acknowledges that new meanings can occur by looking at faith's documents in new ways. These new ways of looking vary widely and can come from anyone.

Listen to the language used by John's Jesus:

> "I am the way, the truth, and the life. No one comes to the Father except through me. If you know me, you will know my Father also. From now on you do know him and have seen him. . . . Whoever has seen me has seen the Father. . . . The words that I say to you I do not speak on my own; but the Father who dwells in me does his works. Believe me that I am in the Father and the Father is in me; but if you do not, then believe me because of the works themselves. Very truly, I tell you, the one who believes in me will also do the works that I do and, in fact, will do greater works than these, because I am going to the Father. I will do whatever you ask in my name. . . . If in my name you ask me for anything, I will do it."

> Here, the Existential View of the Atonement is at work. Instead of being provided with a propositional statement about belief ("Some are saved, but not others"), the disciples are grasped by a sublime experience of God's redemptive power.

Sublime words, majestic, elevated . . . even transported words of inspiration and hope . . . spoken by a Jesus who, at the time of the writing of John's Gospel, is way above and beyond history, way above and beyond the ordinary world of Jesus' historical followers . . . a resurrected and ascended Jesus who is far larger than life and even larger than death. John's hearers, and people like me at my father's funeral, can hear these words and understand.

Look again at what is happening—in, under, and around these words. Jesus is comforting, offering hope, and finally *inspiring* his disciples, John's church, and us today to continue his work in the world—to do greater works. And again, what is that work?

It is the work of offering a comforting and inspiring welcome to fearful, desperate, and troubled people—of inviting them to accompany us into an infinite habitat with many dwelling places. Not the work of slicing up a finite religious or theological pie and serving it to those of our own choosing. Not the work of including people inasmuch as they think, act, or love the way that we do. No, our greater work is to get into the welcome-wagon business—of preparing the way and welcoming people to go with us into God's habitat. And inasmuch as we do this, we too can say with assurance that Christ is *in us,* and that we are *in Christ.* And we can say that no one comes to God except through the experience of a welcoming work—through a voice and a touch that opens the world up to God—

> Here the preacher is moving from a strictly Existential and individualistic understanding of redemption (having a personal experience of God's acceptance, forgiveness, and so on) to a Relational understanding in which God's redemptive power is experienced in the welcoming of the church. Ideas do not save us, only a relational and experiential participation in God's redemptive welcoming power in the church.

through a welcoming agent who can lead a person to the dwelling place *that we know about*—the one where Christ is. Think of all of those who have done this greater work in your life—who rolled out God's welcome wagon for you when you were troubled . . . a parent? A friend? A teacher? A pastor? A stranger?

And so, take comfort and find hope from these sublime words. The habitat-welcoming God has a huge house with many dwelling places. And the one who first welcomed *us*—Jesus of Nazareth—has gone to prepare a place for us and for others whom we welcome "in him," a place where Christ is waiting for

> The preacher now returns to the question of how Christianity relates to other religions. At the very least, he remains open to some form of pluralism—perhaps Radical Pluralism?—without spelling it out. The congregation is urged to attend primarily to their own practices of welcoming.

us. Christ is the way, the truth, and the life *whom we know* . . . the way, truth, and life of infinite, indefinite welcoming that shatters every system of "who's in" and "who's out." It is the presence of this Christ "in us" today that, I hope, will inspire us to even greater works of welcoming in this very troubled world.

In closing, let me make one final comment. We can only welcome to the dwelling place that we know about, the one where Christ has gone to prepare for us, but that is okay and that is enough. As far as I can tell from this story, it is in the very nature of this habitat-welcoming God of many rooms to take care of the rest.

The Theological Profile (Short Form)

I. The Four Basic Theological Modes

1. *The existential mode*: Theology begins with the negativities of existence and finds God as the answer to our self-despair and the ground of life's purpose and meaning.
2. *The transcendent mode*: Theology begins with God's self-revelation, which alone provides true knowledge of God and self, leading us toward a life of proclamation and ministry.
3. *The ethical-political mode*: Theology begins with the fusion of faith and social commitment and finds God's presence in the church's struggle for a just society.
4. *The relational mode*: Theology begins with the connectedness of all things and finds God calling life toward greater degrees of creativity, harmony, and justice.

II. Authority

The authority of the Bible: four types

1. *The way of verbal inspiration*: Scripture is God-speech, transcribed by the biblical writers.
2. *The way of God's uniquely revealed word*: Scripture is the unique witness to divine revelation.
3. *The way of universal principles*: Scripture's narratives, prophetic texts, and so on embed universal truths and ethical principles.
4. *The way of God's fresh address*: Scripture provides God's fresh word to our situations via its openness to new interpretations.

The authority of tradition: three types

1. *Limited absoluteness*: The church has the authority to grant absolute validity to (some of) its traditional teachings and practices.

2. *Limited relativity*: The church's teachings and practices are, in part, conditioned by time and place. Changing social conditions can make some traditions irrelevant and bring to light new truths of our faith.
3. *Absolute relativity*: No church tradition is valid unless authorized by Scripture.

The authority of experience: three types
1. *Absolute denial*: Experience lacks all authority in relation to religious knowledge.
2. *Relative denial*: Apart from faith, experience lacks authority.
3. *Relative affirmation*: Though sin can distort experience, it does not destroy our capacity to experience God's presence, power, and love.

The authority of reason: five types
1. *The way of opposition*: Reason has no authority; its use in theology can only lead to false belief.
2. *The way of harmony*: Reason and faith work together to discover the ultimate truths of God and existence.
3. *The way of hierarchical order*: Reason uncovers general religious truths but needs faith for the highest truths of religion.
4. *The way of dialectical tension*: Reason can bring us to the threshold of faith, but is dangerous if its limits are not recognized.
5. *The way of mutual transformation*: Faith and reason(ing in faith) mutually modify each other in an ongoing way.

III. Theistic Worldviews: five types
1. *Omnipotent theism*: God is the invulnerable power determining the world's determinations.
2. *Supernaturalistic theism*: God has all-determining, invulnerable power but grants the creation human freedom and its own systemic order, intervening in a determinative way only at will.
3. *Pantheism*: God is the invulnerable, determinative order of the particulars (the creatures) of the world.
4. *Relational theism*: God is the vulnerable, necessary, though not determinative, power in the world, affected by and affecting the world.
5. *Natural theism*: God has created a self-sustaining world of good and evil, freely energized by the moral imperative divinely built into the nature of things.

IV. Theodicy: three models

1. *Unlimited dominion*: God controls all events; evil is only apparent, working ultimately to fulfill God's good purposes.
2. *Self-limited dominion*: God's power is self-limited, so that we might freely come to a mature love of God. Evil comes in the back door of our freedom, though it contributes to the maturing process.
3. *Limited dominion*: God's power is maximal, drawing us always toward the good; but there are in the world many powers for good and evil that bear down upon us and affect our decisions.

V.   The Atonement

1. *Christus Victor*: In a once-for-all event, Christ breaks the power of the demonic over human life.
2. *Satisfaction/substitution*: Christ's death is a once-for-all perfect and sufficient offering to God for our sins.
3. *Exemplar*: Christ is our model: an inspiring example of the life of love and faith.
4. *Existential*: In participating in the death and resurrection of Christ, we participate in that ultimate power which overcomes sin and death.
5. *Relational*: Christ's death reveals God's costly, healing love for us, impelling the formation of the new community in Christ's spirit.

VI. The Church and the World

1. *The church against the world*: Church and world represent two separate and opposing ways of life.
2. *The church with the world*: Christ's teachings, which inspire the work of the church, are in harmony with the highest values of the world.
3. *The church above the world*: The church represents a higher order of values relating to and qualifying the world's lower order of values.
4. *The church and world in paradox*: Church and world values are in conflict with each other; nevertheless, the church participates in secular structures to restrain sin.
5. *The church as transformer of the world*: The church is in an ongoing "yes" and "no" relation to the world, ever calling the world toward further transformation.

VII. The Relation of Christianity to Other Religions

1. *Radical exclusivism* (the way of rejection): God is known through Christ alone; other religions reflect human projections of the divine.
2. *Radical inclusivism* (the way of identity): Religions in their depth are at one; their permanent truths are what they hold in common.
3. *Hierarchical pluralism* (the way of stages): Christianity is the highest religion, though all religions contain some truth.
4. *Radical pluralism* (the way of otherness): Religions are radically and permanently distinct from each other; faith can only be confessional.
5. *Dynamic pluralism* (the way of mutual transformation): Relations modify religions without undermining their distinct identity.

The Relation of Christianity to Judaism

1. *Supersessionism*: Christianity replaces Judaism as the religion of God's covenant people.
2. *Eschatological mysticism*: Judaism remains within God's providential plan, the purpose of which will be revealed in the end.
3. *Forked parallelism*: Ancient Israelite faith forks into (1) Rabbinic Judaism, stressing ancient Israel's particularistic elements; and (2) Christianity, stressing ancient Israel's universalistic elements.

VIII. Endings

The kingdom and the end (aim) of history

1. *Other-worldly*: The kingdom of God is above; life in the world is a necessary, though painful, passageway to eternal blessedness.
2. *Apocalyptic eschatology*: The kingdom of God is coming; God will break into history, destroying the old reality, establishing the new.
3. *Realized eschatology*: The kingdom of God is here, inwardly present to those who walk in the way of the Spirit of Christ.
4. *Dialectical*: The kingdom is present in part (history contains real achievements of justice), is forever coming (there are always old and new injustices to overcome), and is above (fulfillment is only possible beyond history).
5. *Evolutionary*: The kingdom is coming, slowly and with setbacks, but inevitably, as the creation evolves toward the realization of God's aims.

The kingdom and eternal life

1. *Individualistic*: In the kingdom, each person is one among many, distinct, autonomous, and brought to individual perfection.

2. *Communal*: In the kingdom, personal life is brought to perfection through the full communion of person with person.
3. *Mystical*: In the kingdom, we become at one with God, dying to self and to differentiation.
4. *The* via ignota: Knowledge of eternal life lies beyond our grasp; we live in faith that death cannot separate us from God.

Appendix B

Theological Profile Chart

I. Basic Theological Modes	II. Authority	
	Bible	*Tradition*
❑ 1. Existential ❑ 2. Transcendent 　 3. Ethical-Political 　 ❑ Social Gospel 　 ❑ Liberationist ❑ 4. Relational	❑ 1. Verbal Inspiration ❑ 2. Unique Word ❑ 3. Universal Principles ❑ 4. Fresh Address	❑ 1. Limited Absoluteness ❑ 2. Limited Relativity ❑ 3. Absolute Relativity

IV. Theodicy	V. The Atonement	VI. The Church and the World
❑ 1. Unlimited Dominion ❑ 2. Self-limited Dominion ❑ 3. Limited Dominion	❑ 1. Christus Victor ❑ 2. Satisfaction/ Substitution ❑ 3. Exemplar ❑ 4. Existential ❑ 5. Relational	❑ 1. Church against World ❑ 2. Church with World ❑ 3. Church above World ❑ 4. Church and World in Paradox ❑ 5. Church as Transformer of World

III. Theistic World-views

Experience

- ❏ 1. Absolute Denial
- ❏ 2. Relative Denial
- ❏ 3. Relative Affirmation

Reason

- ❏ 1. Opposition
- ❏ 2. Harmony
- ❏ 3. Hierarchical
- ❏ 4. Dialectical
- ❏ 5. Mutual Transformation

- ❏ 1. Omnipotent Theism
- ❏ 2. Supernaturalistic Theism
- ❏ 3. Pantheism
- ❏ 4. Relational Theism
- ❏ 5. Natural Theism

VII. The Relation of Christianity to Other Religions

- ❏ 1. Radical Exclusivism
- ❏ 2. Radical Inclusivism
- ❏ 3. Hierarchical Pluralism
- ❏ 4. Radical Pluralism
- ❏ 5. Dynamic Pluralism

Relation to Judaism

- ❏ 1. Supersessionism
- ❏ 2. Eschatological Mysticism
- ❏ 3. Forked Parallelism

VIII. Endings

The End of History

- ❏ 1. Other-Worldly
- ❏ 2. Apocalyptic Eschatology
- ❏ 3. Realized Eschatology
- ❏ 4. Dialectical
- ❏ 5. Evolutionary

Eternal Life

- ❏ 1. Individualistic
- ❏ 2. Communal
- ❏ 3. Mystical
- ❏ 4. *Via Ignota*

Notes

PART 1: PRELIMINARY REMARKS

1. Cf. Paul Jones, *Theological Worlds: Understanding the Alternative Rhythms of Christian Belief* (Nashville: Abingdon Press, 1989), where all types are interpreted through an existential psychology.

2. Cf. George Lindbeck, *The Nature of Doctrine: Religion and Theology in a Postliberal Age* (Philadelphia: Westminster Press, 1984), where two of the three types are dismissed as invalid.

CHAPTER 1: THE HIDDEN DETERMINANTS

1. Cf. Dietrich Bonhoeffer, *The Cost of Discipleship* (New York: Touchstone, 1995), ch. 12.

2. Ibid., ch. 32.

3. Dietrich Bonhoeffer, *Ethics* (London: SCM Press, 1955), 116.

CHAPTER 2: DOCTRINES

1. Gustaf Aulén, *Christus Victor,* trans. A. G. Hebert (New York: Macmillan Co., 1961).

2. H. Richard Niebuhr, *Christ and Culture* (New York: Harper & Brothers, 1951), esp. ch. 1.

3. The other elements of ancient Israel's faith are still present but in the background. They are, of course, capable of being brought to the fore at auspicious times—the establishment of Israel as a Jewish state revived into power the notion of the promised land and opens up the possibility of rebuilding the temple.

4. *Ignota,* in classical Latin, refers not only to the unfamiliar or the strange but to that which lies beyond our knowledge or experience. Cf. the *Oxford Latin Dictionary,* ed. P. G. W. Glare (Oxford: Clarendon Press, 1982), 285.

CHAPTER 3: THE THEOLOGICAL PROFILE AND SERMON BRAINSTORMING

1. Juan Luis Segundo, *The Liberation of Theology* (Maryknoll, N.Y.: Orbis Books, 1976), 9, quoted in Justo González and Catherine González, *Liberation Preaching: The Pulpit and the Oppressed* (Nashville, Abingdon Press, 1980), 31.